Willie Nelson Family Album

Compiled by

LANA NELSON FOWLER

H.M. Poirot & Company

Amarillo

ACKNOWLEDGMENTS

For the use of their photographs:

Atlantic Records   Scott Newton
Columbia Records   Rosa Nichols
Jasper Dailey   Mark Peel
George Fowler   Stan Rhoden
Kanof   Zavell-Smith
Rich Henson   Melinda Wichman
Les Leverett   The White House
Libby Leverett

For the use of previously published material:

Buddy Magazine   *Texas Monthly*
Cashbox   Jay Milner
Dallas Times Herald   Crash Stewart

For the use of Willie Nelson's songs:

Columbia Pictures, Inc.   Willie Nelson Music Company

Designed by John C. Nye
Calligraphy and etchings by Martha Hannah
Hand-tooling and cover design by Paul English
Printed in the United States of America at Kingsport, Tennessee
First edition: September 1980

Copyright © 1980 by Lana Nelson Fowler
Published by H.M. Poirot & Company,
P.O. Box 30171, Amarillo, Texas 79120

Library of Congress Catalog Number: 80-80523
International Standard Book Number: 0-936318-00-7

We all loved you
and dedicate this Family Album
to you, Mama Nelson.

The following special people helped to make this book come together:

Aunt Rosie	Mama	Jody
Moody	Paul	Lee
Mildred	Jeanne	Stephanie
Mama Nelson	Scott	Grandma Harvey
Randy and Phyllis	Lorraine	Aunt Bobbie

Foreword

In 1975 when my sister Mary Christine and her friend Lana Nelson were sharing a house near Buda, Texas, I saw several family scrapbooks that gave a quick and true glimpse into the life of Willie Nelson. Lana mentioned her desire to someday publish a family album that would include family, friends, significant events, and her father's song lyrics. We all talked of the possibility.

Three years later we agreed that the time had arrived. I encouraged Lana to consolidate her scrapbooks and to prepare a single volume that would eventually become *Willie Nelson Family Album.* After Lana asked Paul English to design and hand-tool a leather cover, we decided to present the finished book to Willie as a surprise on his forty-seventh birthday, April 30, 1980.

This book is a brief record of what one man has chosen to do with his life. I like to think that Willie's life and this book make a positive statement about family and friends and the passage of time. For without the help of family and friends and the passage of time, this book would not be.

I want to thank Lana and Mary. I also want to thank Janice Picone, Patty Mittelstadt, Jack Nye, L. Dean Cobb, William F. Dunn, III, David Hays, Tony Matteson, Milton Walker, Dewayne Weatherly, Paul English, and Willie Nelson.

H. M. Poirot
January 1, 1980

Preface

The one and only reason that I put this book together
was to do something special for my father
and to share with everyone the love we all have.

LANA NELSON FOWLER

CHAPTER 1

The Time Is April

You Do Know Why You're Here

Yes, there's great confusion on earth, and the power
that is has concluded the following:
Perfect man has visited earth already and his voice was heard;
The voice of imperfect man must now be made manifest
And I have been selected as the most likely candidate.

YES, THE TIME IS APRIL, AND THEREFORE YOU,
A TAURUS, MUST GO.
TO BE BORN UNDER THE SAME SIGN TWICE
ADDS STRENGTH AND THIS STRENGTH, COMBINED WITH
WISDOM AND LOVE, IS THE KEY.

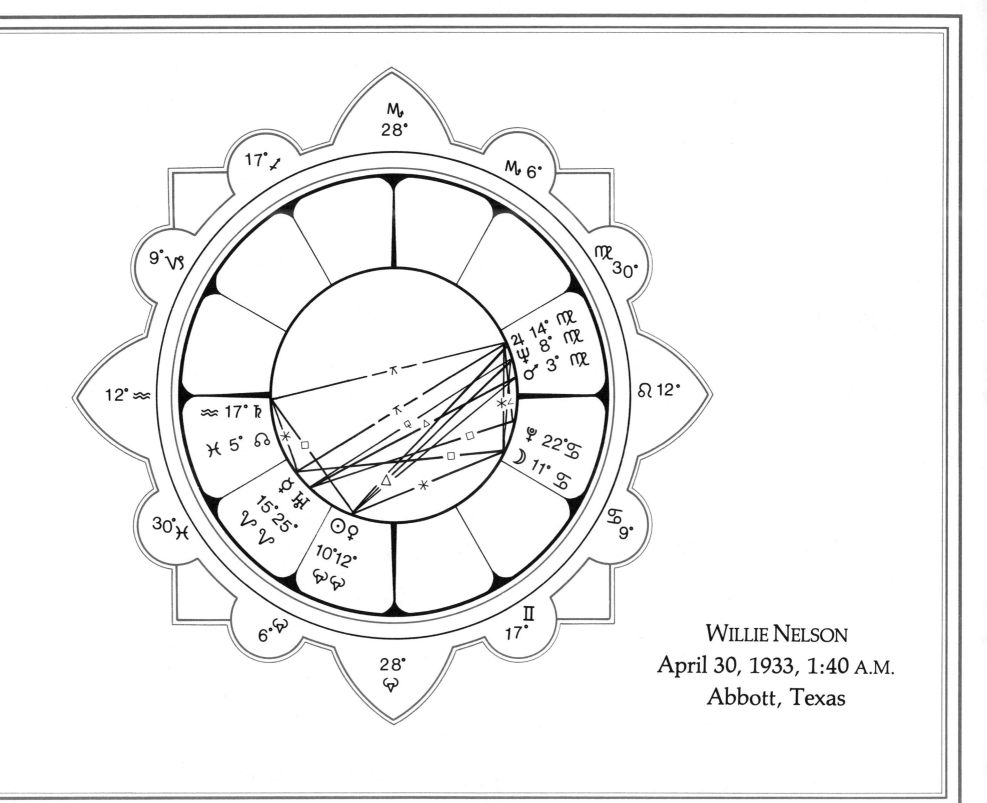

WILLIE NELSON
April 30, 1933, 1:40 A.M.
Abbott, Texas

Let Me Be a Man

Explain to me again, Lord, why I'm here;
I don't know, I don't know.
The setting for the stage is still not clear;
Where's the show? Where's the show?
Let it begin, let it begin.
I am born. Can you use me?

What would you have me to do, Lord?
Shall I sing them a song?
I could tell them all about you, Lord;
I could sing of the loves I have known.

I'll work in their cotton and corn field;
I promise to do all I can;
I'll laugh and I'll cry, I'll live and I'll die.

Please, Lord, let me be a man,
And I'll give it all that I can.
If I'm needed in this distant land,
Please, Lord, let me be a man.

Before I begin this elaborate journey
Portraying earth's typical man,
Last minute instructions would surely be welcome;
Please, Lord, let me hold to your hand.

Dear Lord, let me be a man
And I'll give it all that I can.
If I'm needed in this distant land,
Please, Lord, let me be a man.

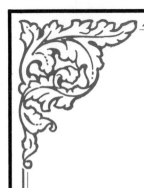

In 1900, on a winter day in Marion County, Arkansas,
William Alfred Nelson married Nancy Elizabeth Smothers.
They spent their early married years homesteading forty
acres of land in Searcy County, Arkansas, two and
one-half miles from Pindall. They had three children: Clara, Rosa,
and a son named Ira.

Nancy Elizabeth Smothers and
William Alfred Nelson
"Mama and Daddy Nelson"
Marion County, Arkansas, 1929

Ira Doyle Nelson, Arkansas, 1915

Ira and his cousin, Fred Smothers

Ira and Myrle

In 1929, Ira married Myrle Greenhow in Pindall and moved from Arkansas to Abbott, Texas with Mama and Daddy Nelson. Daddy Nelson made a living as a blacksmith in Abbott and everyone in the family was an active member of the Abbott Methodist Church. Ira and Myrle had two children: a daughter, Bobbie Lee, and a son, Willie Hugh.

When Bobbie was five and Willie was two, Ira and Myrle separated and were soon divorced. Myrle then married Ken Harvey and moved to Oregon; Ira married Lorraine Moon and moved to Fort Worth where they had two sons, Charles and Doyle.

This left Willie and Bobbie to be raised by Mama and Daddy Nelson, their grandparents.

"Mama and Daddy Nelson both were great musicians and had mail order music degrees.

"Mama Nelson used to say that music was anything that sounded good to the ear.

"Daddy Nelson was a blacksmith in Abbott until he died when I was six. He had already taught me a few chords on the guitar."

Family Bible

There's a Family Bible on the table
Its pages worn and hard to read,
But the Family Bible on the table
Will ever be my key to memories.

At the end of day when work was over
And when the evening meal was done,
Dad would read to us from the Family Bible
And we'd count our many blessings one by one.

I can see us sitting 'round the table
When from the Family Bible Dad would read,
And I can hear my mother softly singing
Rock of Ages, Rock of Ages, Cleft for me.

Now this old world of ours is filled with trouble.
This old world would oh so better be
If we found more Bibles on the table
And mothers singing Rock of Ages, Cleft for me.

I can see us sitting 'round the table
When from the Family Bible Dad would read,
And I can hear my mother softly singing
Rock of Ages, Rock of Ages, Cleft for me.

Bobbie and Willie, 1935

Bobbie, Doyle, and Willie Nelson

Taken at a family picnic at Cameron Park in Waco, Texas

Bobbie, Doyle, and Willie

Sybil, Bobbie, Mama Nelson, Willie, and Ernestine, with Doyle in front

Lorraine and Ira Nelson

Willie Nelson, Abbott High Panthers, 1948

Willie Hugh Nelson

Willie and Mama Nelson, Waco, Texas, 1950

CHAPTER
2

Remember the Good Times

Bobbie learned to play piano and read music from Mama Nelson. She became a piano teacher herself while still in high school. Willie, taking the chords he had learned from Daddy Nelson, taught himself to play the guitar. Willie was ten years old when he got his first paying job with a polka band.

Bobbie got married in 1955 to Bud Fletcher, also a musician. Willie and Bobbie, with a few other friends played in Bud's band.

Willie and Bobbie at left, Bud, playing fiddle, and Ira "Pop" Nelson at right.

Joe Massey and the Frontiersmen

Remember the Good Times

Remember the good times;
They're smaller in number, and easier to recall.
Don't spend too much time on the bad times;
Their staggering number will be heavy as lead on your mind.

Don't waste a moment unhappy;
Invaluable moments, gone with the leakage of time,
As we leave on our own separate journeys,
Movin' west, with the sun, to a place buried deep in our minds.

"My first wife, Martha, was a full-blooded Cherokee Indian.
And every night with us was like Custer's last stand."

In 1952, Willie married Martha Mathews from Waco.

Summer of Roses

A short time I have to be with you, my love,
But a short time is better than no time, you see;
So I bring to you all my possessions
And would that you'd share them with me.

I bring you one springtime of robins,
A springtime of robins to sing;
I bring to you one summer of roses,
One summer of roses I bring.

I bring to you one autumn of dry leaves,
Dry leaves will be helpful, you see,
To soften the fall of your snowflakes
When I bring you your winter of snow.

By 1958, Willie and Martha had three children.

Lana, Susie, and Billy Nelson

In God's Eyes

Never think evil thoughts of anyone;
It's just as wrong to think as to say,
For a thought is but a word that's unspoken;
In God's eyes, He sees it this way.

In God's eyes, we're like sheep in a meadow;
Now and then a lamb goes astray,
But open arms should await his returning;
In God's eyes, He sees it this way.

"I was a Sunday School teacher in the Metropolitan Baptist Church in Fort Worth, Texas, at one time. Someone in the congregation found out that I was a musician and that I played in nightclubs all over Texas, and, to this person, this was not a respectable way to make a living. So he mentioned it to the pastor, and he came to me and said there had been a complaint in the church because I was out in these sin holes, playing and singing for all these crazy people in these beer joints, which I was! But the funny part of it was that I was singing to the same people Sunday morning! I ran into a lot of the same faces Saturday and Sunday. They told me that I had to either quit the joints or quit the church. And the church wasn't paying near as much as the clubs were, and I was trying to support my family at the time. I think that this person that was complaining was a person who put a lot of money into the church every Sunday, and the Pastor may have said, Do I want this broke picker or do I want this person who throws money into the church?' I'm not saying that this is what happened, but, if it did, then he took his money and I took mine. We just got them in different places. I've never belonged to a church since then. I've been to church, but not a great deal. This kind of turned me against organized religions. In other words, the plumbers and the electricians could go in there and do their work and it was okay, but I couldn't; so I took this as an attack on me personally; so I left the church. I don't have any feelings for this person now. I think that he felt that the image he wanted in his church wasn't anything like what I looked like and what I did."

It's Not for Me to Understand

I passed a home the other day
And the yard was filled with kids at play;
And on the sidewalk of this home
A little boy stood all alone.

His smiling face was sweet and kind,
But I could see the boy was blind;
He listened to the children play,
I bowed my head and there I prayed.

Dear Lord above, why must this be?
And then these words came down to me:
After all, you're just a man
And it's not for you to understand.

It's not for you to reason why,
You too are blind without my eyes;
So question not what I command,
'Cause it's not for you to understand.

Now when I pray, my prayer is one,
I pray his will, not mine, be done.
After all, I'm just a man;
It's not for me to understand.

Willie

Your old cotton pickin', snuff dippin', tobaccer chewin', stump jumpin', gravy soppin', coffee-pot dodgin', dumplin' eatin', frog giggin', hillbilly from Hill County . . .

WILLIE NELSON

"I first met Paul in Fort Worth in 1954. I was a disc jockey there and I had a daily radio program, where I would pick and sing for about thirty minutes. Paul's brother Oliver was a drummer, and I sang and played guitar. One day Oliver couldn't make it, and so Paul played that day. It's the first time that he'd ever played in his life. He'd been playing trumpet in the Salvation Army. We told him when to hit, and we got the beat started for him. Obviously, he had some hidden natural talent, and he picked it right up."

Paul English

CHAPTER

3

I Guess Nashville Was the Roughest

In 1960, Willie, Martha, and the three children moved to Nashville. Willie sang his songs to anyone who would listen. Soon, he had a writing contract and his songs were published through Pamper Music Company. Martha took a job as a night bartender at the Wagon Wheel downtown, while Willie babysat at home. Later, Willie started playing bass with Ray Price and fronting his band. Faron Young cut "Hello Walls" and it was a hit. Patsy Cline cut "Crazy" followed up by Billy Walker's first version of "Funny How Time Slips Away."

Night Life

When the evening sun goes down
You will find me hangin' 'round;
The night life ain't a good life,
But it's my life.

Many people just like me,
Dreamin' of old used to be's.
The night life ain't a good life,
But it's my life.

Listen to the blues that they're playin'
Listen to what the blues are sayin'
My, it's just another scene
From the world of broken dreams;
The night life ain't a good life,
But it's my life.

"When I got to Nashville, I tried out for the job of playing bass for Ray Price. Johnny Paycheck had just quit, and Ray needed a bassman. But I didn't know a thing about playing the bass; I had never even picked one up before. Luckily, I picked it up pretty quick."

Hello Walls

Hello walls.
How'd things go for you today?
Don't you miss her
Since she up and walked away?

I'll bet you dread to spend another lonely night with me
But, lonely walls, I'll keep you company.

She went away, and left us all alone the way she planned.
Guess we'll have to get along without her if we can.

Hello window.
Well I see that you're still here.
Aren't you lonely
Since our darling disappeared?

Look here. Is that a teardrop in the corner of your pane?
Now don't you try and tell me that it's rain.

She went away and left us all alone the way she planned.
Guess we'll have to get along without her if we can.

Hello ceiling.
I'm gonna stare at you awhile.
You know I can't sleep;
So won't you bear with me awhile.

We gotta all stick together
Or else I'll lose my mind.
I got a feeling she'll be gone a long, long time.

Funny How Time Slips Away

Well, hello there, my it's been a long, long time.
"How'm I doin?" Oh, I guess that I'm doin' fine.
It's been so long now and it seems that it was only yesterday.
Gee, ain't it funny how time slips away.

How's your new love, I hope that he's doin' fine.
Heard you told him that you'd love him till the end of time.
Now, that's the same thing that you told me, seems like only yesterday.
Gee, ain't it funny how time slips away.

Got to go now, guess I'll see you around.
Don't know when tho', never know when I'll be back in town.
But remember what I tell you, that in time you're gonna pay.
And it's surprising how time slips away.

Crazy

Crazy, crazy for feelin' so lonely.
I'm crazy, crazy for feelin' so blue.
I knew you'd love me as long as you wanted,
And then someday you'd leave me for somebody new.

Worry, why do I let myself worry?
Wond'rin' what in the world did I do.

Crazy for thinking that my love could hold you.
I'm crazy for tryin' crazy for cryin',
And I'm crazy for lovin' you!

In October of 1963, Willie and Martha were divorced in Nashville, Tennessee. Martha took the children and moved to Las Vegas, Nevada, then to Los Angeles, California, and finally back to Waco, Texas.

"I was on the road a lot and away from Martha. She couldn't handle the way we were living; so we got a divorce."

Little Things

I hope I won't disturb you with this call,
I'm just in town for just a little while;
And I thought perhaps you'd like to hear the news,
Jeannie's grades were the highest in the school.
Billy sure does look a lot like you,
I understand your other son does too;
And Billy said, "Tell Mom I miss her so,"
These were some little things I thought you'd like to know.

Remember Sam and Peg who lived next door,
With them it seemed we always laughed so much;
Well Sam and Peg don't live there anymore,
I understand they broke up just like us.
The house we lived in now has been torn down,
Of all the things we owned the last to go;
A freeway now runs through that part of town,
These were some little things I thought you'd like to know.

May 28, 1963

My Dearest Children,

Well here I am again, your great big, fat, ugly daddy missing you very much. It seems that everything I turn around and every where I look, I see some little boy playing with his ball or little girls dressed up so pretty walking down the street and I think of you.

As you grow older, you will come to realize that things do not always work out exactly as you want them to. There will be many things that you will want more than anything in the world but for some reason you wont be able to have them. Then you may feel badly and think that life has played a dirty trick on you and you will not be able to understand why. But always stop and remember what Daddy told you, happiness does not come from having everything you want, but in understanding and accepting all, and in prayer and the belief that every thing always happens for the best. Always.

Write me soon. I am always looking for your letters.

All the Love in the world

Daddy —

Darkness on the Face of the Earth

The morning that you left me was just another day.
How could I see the sorrow that had found me?
And then you laughed and told me that I was in your way,
And I turned and ran as heaven fell around me.

I stumbled through the darkness; my footsteps were unsure;
I lived within a world that had no sunshine.
When you left me darlin', my world came to an end,
And there was darkness on the face of the earth.

The stars fell out of heaven; the moon could not be found;
The sun was in a million pieces scattered all around.
Why did you ever leave me? you knew how it would hurt,
And now there's darkness on the face of the earth.

You Left a Long, Long Time Ago

You tell me today that you're leaving,
But just think awhile, I'm sure that you must know;
Today might be the day that you walk away,
But you left me a long, long time ago.
Today's just the day that ends it all,
Except the usual memories that always linger on.
And today might be the day that you walk away,
But you left me a long, long time ago.

I stood with helpless hands and watched me lose your love,
A little more each day, then it was gone,
And I kept wond'rin just how long until this day would come,
Just how long could your pride keep hangin' on.
So please don't say you're sorry; don't say anything.
Don't try to say why you must leave; just go.
And today might be the day that you walk away,
But you left me a long, long time ago.

I've Got a Wonderful Future Behind Me

Today as I walk through my garden of dreams,
I'm alone in the sweet used to be.
My past and my present are one and the same,
And the future holds nothing for me.
Yesterday's memories still find me;
Scenes from the past keep returning;
I've got a wonderful future behind me.

You say there is happiness waiting for me,
But I know this is just fantasy;
So I'll trade new tomorrows for old yesterdays,
And live in my garden of dreams.
Yesterday's kisses still burning,
Yesterday's memories still find me;
Scenes from the past keep returning;
I've got a wonderful future behind me.

So Much to Do

My oatmeal tastes just like confetti,
The coffee's too strong, so forget it;
The toast is burning, well, let it!
There's just so much to do since you're gone,
Too much to do all alone.

My tie's lost, I can't find my sweater;
There's the doorbell, I hope that's your letter;
My head aches, I hope I feel better.
There's just so much to do since you're gone,
Too much to do all alone.

So much to do since you're gone,
Too much to do all alone;
And time, time rolls on like a river,
And oh, there's just so much to do,
And I just can't do without you.

Touch Me

Touch me; touch the hand of a man who once owned all the world.
Touch me; touch the arms that once held all the charms of the world's sweetest girl.
Touch me; maybe someday you may need to know how it feels when you lose.
Touch me, and you'll know how you'd feel with the blues.

Watch me; watch the eyes that have seen all the heartbreak and pain in the land.
Be thankful that you're happy, though standing so close to the world's bluest man.
Don't forget me; take a good look at someone who's lost everything he can lose.
Touch me, and you'll know how you'd feel with the blues.

Stay Away from Lonely Places

Stay away from lonely places, follow the crowd;
Stay around familiar faces, play the music loud;
Be seen at all the parties, dress yourself in style;
Stay away from lonely places, for awhile.

Stay away from lonely places 'til you learn to live alone,
Someone's outstretched arms are waiting to stay with you at least 'til dawn;
Remember that sorrow prospers in a heart that never smiles;
So stay away from lonely places, for awhile.

It Should Be Easier Now

Now that I've made up my mind, you're gone,
It should be easier now.
Perhaps now my heart will stop hangin' on;
It should be easier now.
The lesson I learned from you gold can't buy:
A heart can be broken and still survive.
Thanks to you now a much wiser man am I;
It should be easier now.

The worst now is over. I stood the test;
It should be easier now.
They say everything happens for the best;
It should be easier now.
The wounds in my heart you've carved deep and wide,
Hollowed and washed with the tears I cried,
But now there will be more room for love inside;
It should be easier now.

Healing Hands of Time

They're working while I'm missing you,
Those healing hands of time.
Soon they'll be dismissing you
From this heart of mine.
They'll lead me safely through the night,
And I'll follow as though blind;
My future tightly clutched within those healing hands of time.

They let me close my eyes just then,
Those healing hands of time.
Soon they'll let me sleep again,
Those healing hands of time.
So already I've reached mountain peaks,
And I've just begun to climb;
I'll get over you by clinging to those healing hands of time.

"After Martha, I married Shirley Collie. She was a singer and yodeler on the Louisiana Hayride when we met. After we married, we moved to Ridgetop, Tennessee, and bought a farm, where I attempted to be a part-time hog farmer. I was the worst hog farmer you ever saw."

Shirley Collie Nelson, 1965

"Ray Price used to have some fighting roosters back earlier in his career. He lived in Hendersonville, and I lived in Ridgetop, Tennessee. I had a farm, and Ray called one day and asked if he could use my place to walk some of his roosters, to exercise them, and he wanted to try one out on my farm. I said, 'Sure, but he won't hurt any of my laying hens that I've got out there.' He assured me that he wouldn't hurt them, and brought him out. We had eight, and my wife, Shirley, had everyone of them named. About two days after he brought him out, I went out there and one of my hens was dead. I called Ray and said, 'You had better come and get this rooster 'cause he's already killed one of Shirley's hens.' He said, 'Okay, I'll come out and get the rooster and bring another hen.' Well, three weeks went by, and Shirley got up and went out and there was another dead hen. Shirley was really hot now, and she was going to go and shoot the rooster. I said, 'No, let me,' 'cause I didn't like the idea of her alone out there with a loaded shotgun around the horses and cattle in the barn. So I went out and shot the rooster and gave it to Pearl, our housekeeper, for dinner. I called Ray and he said, 'You just killed a thousand dollar rooster.' I said, 'There ain't no fighting rooster in the world worth one good laying hen.' "

"In the Milwaukee airport, Paul had left his briefcase in the taxi, and I had run back to get it. He mentioned it to one of the airport employees, asking if maybe they could sabotage one of the engines 'til Willie can get here. The next thing I know, I'm running back with the briefcase and run into about twenty policemen, who had gathered around Paul. After a few hours, they let us go. I think that they finally figured out that we were only trying to get out of there."

Paul English, Willie, Jimmy Day, David Zentner

Me and Paul

It's been rough and rocky travelin', but I'm finally standin' upright on the ground;
After takin' several readings,
I'm surprised to find my mind still fairly sound;
I guess Nashville was the roughest, but I know I said the same about them all;
We received our education,
In the cities of the nation, me and Paul.

Almost busted in Laredo, but for reasons that I'd rather not disclose;
But, if you're stayin' in a motel there and leave,
Just don't leave nothin' in your clothes;
And, at the airport in Milwaukee, they refused to let us board the plane at all;
They said we looked suspicious,
But I believe they liked to pick on me and Paul.

On a package show in Buffalo, with us and Kitty Wells and Charlie Pride,
The show was long and we're just sittin' there,
And we'd come to play and not just for the ride,
Well, we drank a lot of whiskey, so I don't know if we went on that night at all;
I don't think they even missed us;
I guess Buffalo ain't geared for me and Paul.

It's been rough and rocky travelin', but I'm finally standin' upright on the ground;
After takin' several readings,
I'm surprised to find my mind still fairly sound;
I guess Nashville was the roughest, but I know I said the same about them all;
We received our education,
In the cities of the nation, me and Paul.

"the Devil"

During Willie's ten-year stay in Nashville, he
recorded about a dozen albums, two on
Liberty and the rest on RCA Victor and
Atlantic. On November 24, 1964, he signed
with the famed Grand Ole Opry. He received
several awards from the industry, became
fed up with the politics of becoming a star in
Nashville, and moved home to Texas.

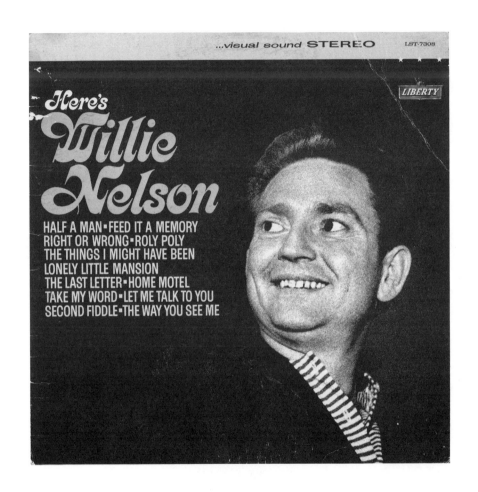

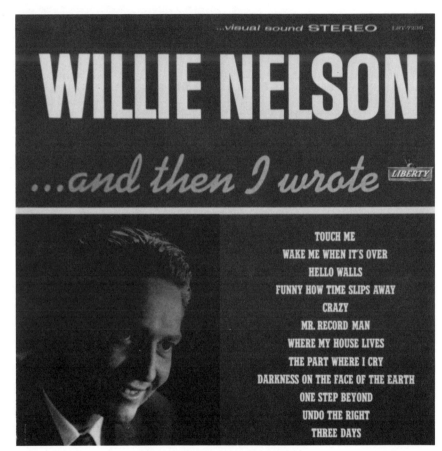

Willie's first two albums, on Liberty Records, 1961

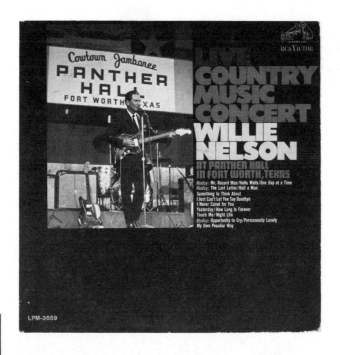

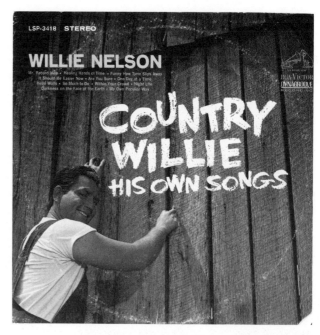

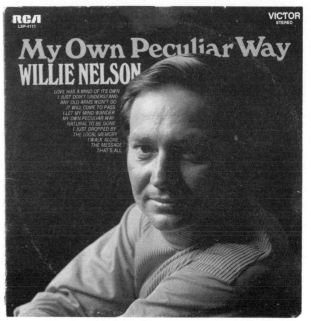

Willie signing with the Grand Ole Opry, November 24, 1964

First time on the Grand Ole Opry as a cast member, November 28, 1964

January 6, 1965

WILLIE

By CRASH STEWART

Before Willie and Shirley divorced, Ray Price and I were planning a Texas tour, and I was in Nashville discussing the details of the tour when Price got a fantastic offer to tour up north for a promoter named Abe Hamza.

Price reluctantly told me for financial reasons he must take the Hamza tour. Willie jumped up and said to me, "I will take Price's place."

I said O.K., but told Willie he was not equal to Price at this stage of his career. Willie said "I know that, but we will hire another big star to replace Price and call it the Willie Nelson show starring the other names who are actually better known than I am."

The artist we chose to replace Price was Marty Robbins. And on the same tour we hired Charlie Pride and gave him his first touring job. Willie heard Charlie sing and he agreed that I was right. Stonewall Jackson, Jeannie Sealy, Hank Cochran and Johnny Bush were the other artists on the tour.

After the Texas tour it was Willie's idea that I start booking from my finance company office in San Antonio. We formed a partnership, which lasted for five years and I can honestly say that Willie and I never had a cross word.

My first agreement with Willie was that I had to get $400 a night for Willie and the band on a week night, $500 on a Friday or Sunday and $600 on a Saturday night.

Our first engagement was at the VFW Hall in Alice, which we had to promote ourselves. We came out OK on the date and never looked back. One of our next dates was a dance at the Melody Ranch in San Antonio.

The members of the band at this stage were Jimmy Day on steel guitar, Wade Ray on fiddle and Johnny Bush on base and drums. The other drummer's name escapes me.

The Willie Nelson and Johnny Bush era was hilarious. They would be in San Antonio and get a job in Houston, for instance, and not have the money to get there, so they would hock their guitars to have gas money and when they got there they would have to borrow a guitar.

About that time, Willie worked as a door-to-door salesman selling encyclopedias, which Willie told me he enjoyed very much.

Willie also worked as a disc jockey and salesman for KIKK in Houston, and Willie will openly tell you that he was fired because he could not pick and sing at night and get up in time to do his morning radio spot.

Leroy Gloger, who at that time was the owner of KIKK, has had many a laugh with Willie over his firing.

One thing about Willie is that if you were right and you had to make a decision that went against Willie, then he would understand. However, you better be right because Willie is strong-minded.

When Willie and Bush were both working at KBOP in Pleasanton as disc jockeys, they were picking and singing around San Antonio and one morning Bush ran out of gas on the way to work. He had to hitchhike to Pleasanton.

About 3 hours later, Willie was on his way to relieve Bush when he passed Bush's car on the side of the road. About a mile further down the road, Willie ran out of gas.

It is funny in this day and time to look back and realize how two superstars of today did not have the money to buy enough gas to get to their daytime jobs. Doc Parker was the owner of KBOP at the time.

Another funny story that Willie told me was when he and Bush were hitchhiking to West Texas to play a job and they were not having any luck in catching a ride. About a block away a freight train stopped which was going in their direction.

Willie got the wild idea for him and Bush to hop the freight. As they approached the train, it started moving very slowly. Willie and Bush tossed their luggage on the flat car, then their guitars.

By this time the train was going so fast they could not get aboard and they lost their luggage and their guitars.

On the way back from the same West Texas trip, Willie said the warmest place he found to sleep was a culvert.

Willie and Bush moved all around Texas, mainly between Ft. Worth, Houston, and San Antonio and about this time they were staying in Houston a little bit more because Bush had relatives there and they would always find a hot meal and a warm bed.

Willie's songwriting ability must have rubbed off on Bush as he penned the great song "Whiskey River," which Willie opens his shows with. I feel Willie opens with it as a secret tribute to his friend Bush.

Willie was recording for RCA records at this time and Chet Atkins, the famous guitar player, was Willie's producer and one of the funniest things I ever heard Chet say was, "If Willie Nelson don't make it, there ain't going to be no happening."

Anyway, I was in the studio every time Willie was to make a recording. Although Willie never says much, I could tell he was not happy with the way Chet was recording him.

Most pickers think Willie breaks meter and they will try to hesitate and rush to keep up with his phrasing. They are wrong.

Willie has never broken meter in his life and if the pickers would just pick the song as it is supposed to be Willie will be there at the proper time regardless of his phrasing.

One time I told Willie I was afraid he was too far ahead of his time with his lyrics, and Willie told me he wished the world would hurry up and catch up with him as he needed the money.

Willie is the type of person that all he needs to write a song is one simple thought.

Willie wrote a couple of songs that I had given him the idea by just making a statement. For instance, Willie had asked me to teach him to rope calves, and the first time he made a successful catch I hollered at Willie that it was one in a row.

So he immediately sat down and wrote "That Makes One in a Row."

After Willie had stayed in Nashville for about two years, my phone at home rang one night and it was Willie.

He told me his house had burned down in Nashville and he wanted to come back to Texas and wanted me to find him a house close to a golf course.

I found him a house on the golf course at Lost Valley Ranch in Bandera.

Willie was heartbroken about losing his home, his belongings and about 500 songs he had written which were not yet published.

Willie wasn't in a mood to work much and he asked me to book a few dates for him at John T. Floore's Country Store in Helotes. All Willie wanted to do was make some money to live on and pay the band.

Willie and I decided we wanted to promote some more shows and we got John T. Floore to back us financially. John T. and Willie remained friends until John T's death several years ago. I guess if an entertainer ever had a night club he could call home, Willie would call Floore's Country Store his home.

Chill Wills, Willie, Crash Stewart, Geno McCoslin, early sixties

One Step Beyond

I'm just one step before losing you,
And I'm just one step ahead of the blues;
And I know that there's been pain and misery,
Long before this old world ever heard of me.
And I know it will hurt to see you go,
But we'll just add one more heartache to the score;
And tho' I still love you as before,
I'm just one step beyond caring anymore.

Bet you're surprised that I could feel this way,
After staying home and waiting night and day;
For someone who cares so much for me,
You'd come home just long enough to lie to me.
I don't know just where my feelings changed,
I just know I could never feel the same;
And tho' I still love you as before,
I'm just one step beyond caring anymore.

Willie and Shirley were divorced in 1971.

Pretend I Never Happened

Pretend I never happened;
Erase me from your mind.
You will not want to remember any love as cold as mine.
I'll be leavin' in the mornin' for a place I hope to find.
All the places must be better than the ones I leave behind.
I don't suppose you'll be unhappy;
You'll find ways to spend your time.
But if you ever think about me,
And if I ever cross your mind,
Just pretend I never happened;
Erase me from your mind.
You will not want to remember any love as cold as mine.

Buddy

Laugh with me, buddy, jest with me, buddy,
Don't let her get the best of me, buddy,
Don't ever let me start feelin' lonely.
If I ever needed you, buddy,
You know how I really do, buddy,
Don't ever let me start feelin' lonely.
I cry at the least little thing, buddy,
And I'll die if you mention her name, buddy.
Talk to me, buddy, stay with me, buddy,
Let's don't let her get the best of me, buddy,
Don't ever let me start feelin' lonely.

Let's talk about things as they were, buddy,
Before I got mixed up with her, buddy.
Laugh with me, buddy, jest with me, buddy,
Let's don't let her get the best of me, buddy,
Don't ever let me start feelin' lonely.

I'm a Memory

I'm a game that you used to play;
I'm a plan that you didn't lay so well;
I'm a fire that burns in your mind;
Close your eyes;
I'm a memory.

I'm a love that you bought for a song;
I'm a voice on a green telephone;
I'm a day that lasted so long;
Close your eyes;
I'm a memory.

I'm a dream that comes with the night;
I'm a face that fades with the light;
I'm a tear that falls out of sight;
Close your eyes;
I'm a memory.

Sad Songs and Waltzes

I'm writing a song all about you,
A true song as real as my tears,
But you've no need to fear it, for no one will hear it
'Cause sad songs and waltzes aren't selling this year.

I'll tell all about how you cheated,
I'd like for the whole world to hear;
I'd like to get even with you 'cause you're leavin',
But sad songs and waltzes aren't selling this year.

It's a good thing that I'm not a star,
You don't know how lucky you are;
Tho' my record may say it, no one will play it
'Cause sad songs and waltzes aren't selling this year.

Walkin'

After carefully considerin' the whole situation,
And I stand with my back to the wall,
Walkin' is better than runnin' away,
And crawlin' ain't no good at all.

And if guilt is the question and truth is the answer,
And I been lyin' to me all along,
Then there ain't nothin' worth savin' except one another,
And before you wake up, I'll be gone.

'Cause after carefully considerin' the whole situation,
And I stand with my back to the wall,
Walkin' is better than runnin' away,
And crawlin' ain't no good at all.

CHAPTER
4

We Were Headed Home to Austin

I'm Falling in Love Again

I'm falling in love again;
Never thought I would again;
Never thought I would.
And I may be making mistakes again,
But if I lose or win, how will I know?
How will I know? How will I know? How will I know?
And I'm falling in love again,
And if I lose or win, how will I know?

On April 30, 1971, Willie Hugh Nelson married
Connie Jean Koepke in Las Vegas, Nevada.

My Own Peculiar Way

It would be a comfort to know you never doubt me,
Even tho' I give you cause most ev'ry day;
Sometimes I think that you'd be better off without me,
Although I love you in my own peculiar way.

Don't doubt my love if sometimes my mind should wander
To a suddenly remembered yesterday;
My mind could never stay too long away from you,
Because I love you in my own peculiar way.

And tho' I may not always be the way you'd have me be,
Tho' my faults may grow in number day by day;
Let no one ever say I've ever been untrue,
I'll always love you in my own peculiar way.

Home Is Where You're Happy

This room could not hold me for one short minute.
If you weren't here with me, I'd soon be gone.
That chair is just a chair when you're not in it.
It takes more than rooms and chairs to make a home.

Home is where you're happy, and I'm happy here with you
Or any place on earth where you may be.
Home is where you're happy, just any house will do,
And I'll feel at home as long as you're with me.

And if time should someday cause this house to crumble,
We'll move into another, love and all.
And if time should make your footsteps stumble,
Darlin' I'll be there should you fall.

Home is where you're happy, and I'm happy here with you
Or any place on earth where you should be.
Home is where you're happy, just any house will do,
And I'll feel at home as long as you're with me.

"I wore the hole in my guitar with my fingers and a pick. You aren't supposed to use a pick on those kind of classical guitars, mainly because there's no pick guards and you're liable to wear a hole in it."

"I guess that I was greatly influenced by Floyd Tillman,
Leon Payne, Tommy Duncan, and, of course, Bob Wills."

"There are a lot of guitar players that I have liked.
Hank Sugarfoot Garland, George Barnes, and Eldon Shamblim.
But I guess that Django Reinhart was the Daddy of them all.
I guess that I am more of a Django Reinhart fan than anybody
else, as far as guitar playing goes.

I Still Can't Believe You're Gone

This is the very first time since you left me
That I've tried to put my thoughts in a song,
And all I can hear myself saying
Is I still can't believe that you're gone.

I still can't believe that you'd leave me.
What did I do that was so wrong?
There's just too many unanswered questions,
And I still can't believe that you're gone.

But you're gone, and I'm alone, and I'm still livin'.
I don't like it but I'll take it 'til I'm strong,
And all I can hear myself sayin', baby,
Is I still can't believe that you're gone.

Darreyl Wayne, Paul, and Carleene English

Wake Me When It's Over

Well, I'm getting tired now;
I gotta get some sleep now;
I guess I've been worried much too long,
And don't wake me 'til it's over,
'Til the need for you is gone.

I was so happy before I loved you;
I want to be like I was before;
So don't wake me 'til it's over,
When I won't want you anymore.

My eyes are getting weak now,
I gotta get some sleep now,
I gotta rest my aching head;
I just wanna lay here,
Just let me stay here,
'Til the blues get up and leave my bed.

Goodnight, darlin',
Goodnight, darlin',
Goodnight for evermore,
And don't wake me 'til it's over,
When I won't want you anymore.

The Local Memory

The lights go out each evening at eleven,
And up and down the block there's not a sound;
I close my eyes and search for peaceful slumber,
And just then the local memory comes around.
Piles of blues against the door to make sure sleep don't come no more,
He's the hardest workin' memory in this town;
Turns out happiness again and then lets loneliness back in,
And each night the local memory comes around.

Each day I say tonight I may escape him;
I pretend I'm happy and never ever frown,
But at night I close my eyes and pray sleep finds me,
But again the local memory comes around.
Rids the house of all good news and then sets out my cryin' shoes,
But a faithful memory never lets me down;
We're all up 'til light of day, chasing happiness away,
And each night the local memory comes around.

WILLIE

by Jay Milner
January 1975

One night in 1964, Gene McCoslin, then manager of KNOK radio in Dallas, drove down to the old Sportatorium on Industrial to hear Roger Miller in person. He got there early and was leaning against a post near the back of the barn-like auditorium when Willie Nelson strolled onstage with a guitar and opened the show with an hour of songs.

Just a man and his guitar. Alone on the big stage. Singing "Hello Walls," "Touch Me," "Funny How Time Slips Away," "Night Life," "Crazy," "Half a Man" and other songs he'd written himself.

"Well, he knocked me right out," McCoslin said recently in his cluttered Central Expressway office, where he holds out tenaciously as perhaps the last of the independent music promoters. "I forgot all about Roger Miller and everybody else. When I got a chance, I introduced myself to Willie and told him, tried to tell him, how hard his songs hit me."

Next time Willie came to Dallas McCoslin went to work for him. Gave up a lucrative career in radio management to go on the road with Willie and his band to ride an ancient bus that wasn't air conditioned from coast to coast, to ride herd on a crazy gang of outlaw musicians.

'Willie told me they'd told him in Nashville he was ten years away," McCoslin said. "I told him that was a crock, that if anything it was Nashville that was ten years away. I wasn't into music, understand. I was a super salesman! But Willie Nelson turned me around. . . . He had on a brown suit and a clip-on tie, ferkrissakes! What was I doing being impressed by a little man in a brown suit and clip-on tie?"

Ten years later, McCoslin booked Willie Nelson into that same barn, the Sportatorium, and sold out both times to stomping, yelling, adoring crowds consisting mainly of longhaired, new generation people who wouldn't have been caught dead listening to country music in 1964.

Even in the mid-60s Willie was regarded as something of an outlaw in Nashville. He wasn't an angry man, far from

it. Mainly, he went his own way as he does today. T brass in Music City USA told Willie to forget abou singing career and concentrate on writing songs.

"I'd had a little success as a songwriter. . . . Fur How Time Slips Away' and 'Hello Walls,' and those so came out purty quick after I moved to Nashville.

After that, I could afford to be a little bit independe . . . Since they'd gone for my songs and had particularly gone for my singing—and I knew they wac gonna go for my life style—I figgered one out of th wadn't too bad. . . .

"Fact Faron Young told me one time that what I oug do was jest write the songs and he'd sing 'em. . . . T was before I started recording. . . . Faron'd had ha little success with 'Hello Walls' so I guess he figgered if could keep me on the hill writing there'd never be a W Nelson. . . . "

More and more folks—in and outside Texas—got glad and gladder that, indeed, there is a Willie Nelson today. Y indeed. A Willie Nelson who is fast becoming loved by kinds of fans everywhere for his singing, his songwrit and an almost indefinable something more that he's co to mean to them.

Willie and his band played the rock-orien Troubadour night club in Los Angeles and drew ne capacity crowds all week. One night's audience inclue Bob Dylan and Paul McCartney, who came to listen to man Willie Nelson they'd been hearing so much about fr musicians of all persuasions across the country.

And so it goes . . .

So, what has triggered all this seemingly sudden a uniquely personal interest in, and adoration for, apparently easy-going Texas country picker poet who, t night ten years ago, opened the show for Roger Mi without fanfare, front or back, alone on the old Spor torium stage?

The answer is complex and has to do with the com around of several things, including Willie Nelson's decis

ut three years ago to move back to Texas after cutting at
hville for almost a dozen years.

new breed of country musician had been coming of
a generation young enough and sensitive enough in the
ting '60s to know that country music could be better if it
more than three chords and delved deeper with its
cs than a minnow's plunge.

Willie found a new audience for his music in his own
as back yard; so, he and key members of his band
cked Nashville and moved to Austin. At about the same
e, Willie changed record companies—singing with the
w York City based Atlantic Records. These two,
ost simultaneous, moves meant that at about the same
e, Willie was able to make the kind of music he wanted
aake both live and recorded.

he audience Willie discovered in Texas was ready for
music and lyrics. Consciously or not, they had been
ing ready most of their lives. Willie's music was
cally country, but more. And, from the other
ction, this new, younger audience had been hearing
e of the best of their rock era musical heroes—Dylan,
teful Dead, Byrds, Poco, The Band, Nitty Gritty Dirt
d and others—edging toward their country roots for
e time. But a major problem had been that no
blished country stars had been willing, or able, to
reciate what these young pickers were attempting to
omplish—a new, all-American music, firmly rooted in
and country attitudes and sounds, but improved, not
ted, by sounds and viewpoints from more modern
cts of updated living experiences. There was still in the
osphere the residue of social and political
mentations of the 1960s.

the dozen or so years he operated out of Nashville,
ie became a successful songwriter. But his career as a
er had not developed satisfactorily for him. His songs
e out of gut reactions to personal triumphs and failures,
ate joy and pain. He was a journeyman craftsman, but

he was never able to crank out money-making gimmick
songs like "The Streaker." Not long ago, I asked him about
this and he said: "I can't. . . . I like to make myself
believe that my songs will still be around 500 years from
now, and I wouldn't want the people then to find songs like
that among 'em."

"Not that I don't write bad songs now and then," he
added, revealing the now famous Willie smile. "I do, just
like everybody else. But I try not to let anybody hear
them."

To Willie, writing songs was only half the job.
Interpreting them was important too, and the idea that
other singers would always interpret his songs for most
people became increasingly unacceptable. ("I always
thought I sang purty good.")

So, when he heard one day that his house in Tennessee
had burned to the ground in his absence, Willie decided to
bring it all back home to Texas. That is, he decided to keep
it here. When news of the burnout reached him, Willie and
his family were in temporary residence in guest houses on a
dude ranch near Bandera, Texas. It was the off-season, and
they had taken advantage of the cheaper rent to isolate for a
breather, after a long string of years doing one-nighter
tours and other killing show biz tasks. Also, there were the
continuing frustrations from Nashville's discouraging
attitude about his singing career.

At that time, Willie's immediate "family" included wife
Connie, youngest daughter Paula, longtime drummer and
compadre Paul English and his family, bass picker par
excellence Bee Spears, legendary steel guitar man Jimmy
Day, various other wives, girl friends, drop-outs, drop-ins,
and no telling who all.

Their first gig after the Texas move was at Armadillo
World Headquarters in Austin, the first country music act
to play there. Willie and Paul simply walked in one night
and asked Armadillo honcho Eddie Wilson for the job.
Wilson said something like: "Why not?" Let's see if it
works."

It worked.

In the approximately two years since, Willie's Texas
concerts became legendary existential experiences that
consistently packed honky tonks, ballrooms and
auditoriums of all sizes, shapes and persuasions across the
state—particularly in the vicinities of Austin, Dallas and
Houston.

The damn near incredible intimacy shared by Willie and
hundreds or thousands of individuals in his audiences set
his performances apart—placed them on a lofty level
alone. Others might rev up as much mass energy, but none
could simultaneously plug into so many individual
emotional circuits across the footlights. The cliche, "He's
singing just for me!" might have been invented by a Willie
Nelson fan.

Meantime, Music City began to snap to the Willie Nelson
phenomenon. In November of 1973, the Country Music
Songwriters Association in Nashville inducted Willie into
their Hall of Fame, along with Roger Miller and Harlen
Howard. Soon, everywhere you went in Nashville you
heard Willie's name. Articles began to appear, in and out of
Nashville, about a gang of picker poets called "The
Nashville Outlaws," whose membership included such
imposing names as Kris Kristofferson, Waylon Jennings,
Tompal Glaser, Billy Joe Shaver and, of course, Willie
Nelson.

A writer for the New York Times told of something he
called "Progressive Country Music." He said it was a new,
vital country music, and its creative energy seemed to be
centered around Willie Nelson down in Austin.

And people like Gene McCoslin—who had tuned in on
Willie and was saved a decade ago—weren't surprised to
see the bandwagon rolling.

"I just wonder what the hell took everybody else so
damn long," McCoslin said in his cluttered Dallas office,
trying to pat his head and rub his stomach at the same time
and failing miserably.

Heaven and Hell

Sometimes it's heaven and sometimes it's hell,
And sometimes I don't even know;
Sometimes I take it as far as I can,
And sometimes I don't even go.
My front tracks are bound for a cold water well,
And my back tracks are covered with snow.
And sometimes it's heaven,
And sometimes it's hell,
And sometimes I don't even know.

Heaven ain't walkin' on a street paved with gold,
And hell ain't a mountain of fire;
Heaven is layin' in my sweet baby's arms,
And hell is when baby's not there.
My front tracks are bound for a cold water well,
And my back tracks are covered with snow.
And sometimes it's heaven,
And sometimes it's hell,
And sometimes I don't even know.

Pick Up the Tempo

People are sayin' that time'll take care of people like me
And that I'm livin' too fast,
And they say I can't last for much longer.
But little they see that their thoughts of me is my savior,
And little they know that the beat oughta go just a little faster.
So pick up the tempo just a little and take it on home.
The singer ain't singin',
And the drummer's been draggin' too long.
Time will take care of itself;
So just leave time alone,
And pick up the tempo just a little and take it on home.

Well, I'm wild, and I'm mean;
I'm creatin' a scene;
I'm goin' crazy.
Well, I'm good and I'm bad,
And I'm happy, and I'm sad,
And I'm lazy.
I'm quiet, and I'm loud,
And I'm gath'rin' a crowd,
And I like gravy.
About half off the wall,
But I learned it all
In the Navy.
So pick up the tempo just a little and take it on home.
The singer ain't singin',
And the drummer's been draggin' too long.
Time will take care of itself;
So just leave time alone,
And pick up the tempo just a little and take it on home.

Devil in a Sleeping Bag

We were headed home to Austin;
Caught pneumonia on the road,
Taking it home to Connie and the kids.

A wheel ran off and jumped the railroad,
Then ran through a groc'ry store.
If you want to buy a bus, I'm takin' bids.

And the devil shivered in his sleepin' bag;
He said, "Traveling on the road is such a drag.
If we can make it home by Friday, we can brag."
And the devil shivered in his sleepin' bag.

Well, I just got back from New York City;
Kris and Rita done it all,
Raw perfection there for all the world to see.

Lord, I heard an angel singin'
In the Philharmonic Hall.
Rita Coolidge, Rita Coolidge, cleft for me.

And the devil shivered in his sleepin' bag;
He said, "Traveling on the road is such a drag.
If we can make it home by Friday, we can brag."
And the devil shivered in his sleepin' bag.

P.O. Box 3963
Austin, Texas 78764

FUNNY HOW TIME SLIPS AWAY · THREE DAYS · CRAZY · TOUCH ME · MR. RECORD MAN · HALF A MAN · ONE STEP BEYOND · HELLO WALLS
WAKE ME WHEN IT'S OVER · UNDO THE RIGHT · THE PART WHERE I CRY · WHERE MY HOUSE LIVES · DARKNESS ON THE FACE OF THE EARTH

The Best Of
Willie Nelson

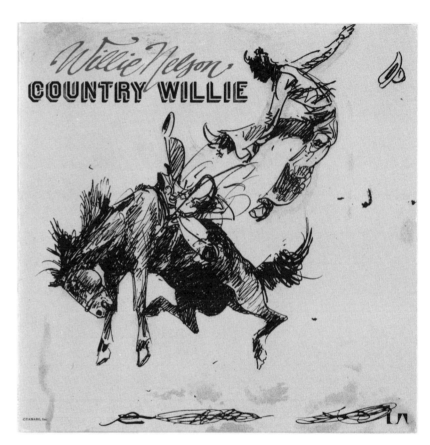

Willie Nelson
COUNTRY WILLIE

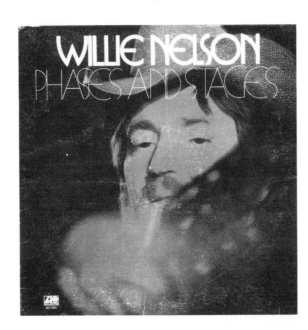

"The best real soul country songs since Hank Williams. . . . At last Willie Nelson is being heard by the public as well as the songwriters who idolize him."

Music City News, September 1973

"A good part of the truth in Willie Nelson's songs comes out when he sings them; his rich baritone comes easing across the room . . . so soulful it's hard not to sing along with him. . . . The honesty in the feeling of his singing and playing make him a country songwriter with instant appeal to a sensitive, curious audience."

Crawdaddy, September 1973

"His deceptively simple lyrics fit whole chapters into single lines. . . . The fact that Nelson can fashion a believable scenario with such sparseness is a tribute to his ability to turn experience into good music."

Rolling Stone, March 14, 1974

"Nelson is writing some of the most amazing songs you ever heard. . . . He makes you listen; what's more, he makes you care."

Hot Wax, San Francisco, April 1974

"Nelson is changing the face of country music. He's making it more acceptable to more people. The interesting thing is that Nelson hasn't changed all that much over the years. It's as if the rest of the country is finally catching up."

The Arizona Republic, May 1974

"Both the music and the lyrics Nelson has written touch us directly because of their genuine concern for the situation that in one form or another strikes many people. . . . [His] albums shine with such soul that only the most extreme hard-rock fanatics could fail to be hooked."

Loraine Alterman, *New York Times*, May 19, 1974

It's Not Supposed to Be That Way

It's not supposed to be that way;
You're supposed to know that I love you.
But it don't matter anyway
If I can't be there to control you.
And, like the other little children,
You're gonna dream a dream or two.
But be careful what you're dreamin',
Or soon your dreams'll be dreamin' you.

It's not supposed to be that way;
You're supposed to know that I love you.
But it don't matter anyway
If I can't be there to console you.
And when you go out to play this evenin',
Play with fireflies 'til they're gone.
And then rush to meet your lover,
And play with real fire 'til the dawn.

December Day

This looks like a December day;
This looks like a time-to-remember day.
And I remember a Spring,
Such a sweet tender thing.
And love's summer college,
Where the green leaves of knowledge
Were waiting to fall with the Fall.
And where September wine
Numbed a measure of time,
Through the tears of October.
Now November's over,
And this looks like a December day.

This looks like a December day;
It looks like we've come to the end of the way.
And as my memories race back to love's eager beginning,
Reluctant to play with the thoughts of the ending,
The ending that won't go away.
And as my memories race back to love's eager beginning,
Reluctant to play with the thoughts of the ending,
The ending that won't go away.
And this looks like a December day.

I Gotta Get Drunk

Well, I gotta get drunk and I sure do dread it,
'Cause I know just what I'm gonna do;
I'll start to spend my money,
Callin' everybody honey,
And wind up singin' the blues.
I'll spend my whole paycheck on some old wreck,
And, brother, I can name you a few;
Well, I gotta get drunk and I sure do dread it,
'Cause I know just what I'm gonna do.

Well, I gotta get drunk; I can't stay sober;
There's a lot of good people in town
Who'd like to hear me holler,
See me spend my dollars,
And I wouldn't think of lettin' em down.
There's a lot of doctors that tell me
That I'd better start slowin' it down!
But there's more old drunks than there are old doctors;
So I guess we'd better have another round.

Shotgun Willie

Shotgun Willie sits around in his underwear,
Bitin' on a bullet and pullin' out all his hair.
Shotgun Willie's got all his family there.

Well, you can't make a record if you ain't got nothin' to say.
You can't make a record if you ain't got nothin' to say.
You can't play music if you don't know nothin' to play.

Now, John T. Floores was working for the Klu Klux Klan.
At six foot five John T. was a hell of a man.
Made alot of money selling sheets on the family plan.

Shotgun Willie sits around in his underwear,
Bitin' on a bullet and pullin' out all his hair.
Shotgun Willie's got all his family there.

Slow Down Old World

Slow down, slow down, old world, there's no hurry,
'Cause my life ain't mine anymore.
I lived too fast; now it's too late to worry
And I'm too blue to cry anymore.

I once was a fool for the women;
Now I'm just a fool, nothing more.
So slow down, slow down, old world, there's no hurry,
'Cause my life ain't mine anymore.

I once had a way with the women,
'Til one got away with my heart.
So slow down, slow down, old world, there's no hurry,
'Cause my life ain't mine anymore.

CHAPTER
5

*We're Aging with Time, like
Yesterday's Wine*

Yesterday's Wine

Miracles appear in the strangest of places;
Fancy meeting you here.
The last time I saw you was just out of Houston;
Sit down and I'll buy you a beer.
Yesterday's wine, I'm yesterday's wine,
Aging with time, like yesterday's wine,
Yesterday's wine, we're yesterday's wine,
Aging with time, like yesterday's wine.

Your presence is welcome with me and my friend here;
This is a hangout of mine.
We come here quite often and listen to music,
Partaking of yesterday's wine.
Yesterday's wine, I'm yesterday's wine,
Aging with time, like yesterday's wine;
Yesterday's wine, we're yesterday's wine,
Aging with time, like yesterday's wine.

You give the appearance of one widely travelled;
I'll bet you've seen things in your time.
So sit down beside me and tell me your story,
If you think you'll like yesterday's wine.
Yesterday's wine, I'm yesterday's wine,
Aging with time, like yesterday's wine;
Yesterday's wine, we're yesterday's wine,
Aging with time, like yesterday's wine.

Willie, 1975

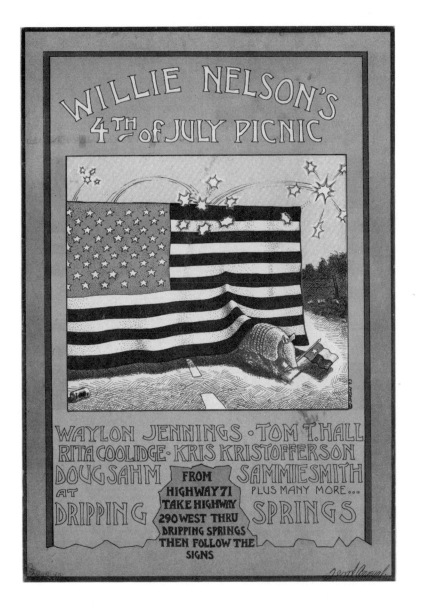

WILLIE NELSON'S
THIRD ANNUAL 4th OF JULY
PICNIC

WILLIE, HIS FAMILY & FRIENDS:

Kris Kristofferson • Rita Coolidge • The Pointer Sisters
The Charlie Daniels Band • Doug Sahm Quintet • Billy Swan
Alex Harvey • Johnny Bush • Donnie Fritts • Billy "C"
Milton Carroll • Delbert McClinton

AT LIBERTY HILL from Austin take Hwy. 183 north then west on Hwy. 29. Tickets $5.50 advance
$7.50 door; Mail Orders: Preston Ticket Agency, P. O. Box 12000, Dallas, Texas 75225.

WILLIE'S FOURTH
FOURTH
OF JULY PICNIC

E PLURIBUS WILLIE

JULY 4,
IN GONZALES
TEXAS

TICKETS AVAILABLE AT:
DALLAS—PRESTON TICKET AGENCY
FT. WORTH—AMUSEMENT TICKET SERVICE
AUSTIN—INNERSANCTUM
HOUSTON—FOLEY'S
SAN ANTONIO—SAN ANTONIO TICKET SERVICE

THE NATIONS'
LARGEST ANNUAL MUSIC EVENT

July 4 Is Picnic Time

Willie Nelson 3d Annual July 4 Picnic Racks Up A 90,000 Gate In Texas

Austin, Texas, July 15.
Willie Nelson and a number of other artists drew a crowd pegged at close to 90,000 for his third annual July 4 picnic in Liberty Hill, around 30 miles north of here. There was an admission charge until the crowd started to pass around 50,000 in the late afternoon and the gates were opened to all gratis.

50,000 Attend Willie Nelson's Annual Picnic

LIBERTY HILL, Tex. (AP) — An estimated 50,000 or more persons swarmed to this tiny Central Texas community Friday for the third annual Willie Nelson 4th of July Picnic, clogging virtually every road leading here, state police said.

Crowds gathering for music

A Patriotic Potpourri on July 4

Refugees, Politicians, Protesters Celebrate

70,000 Watch
Willie At Liberty Hill Bash

Complaints Filed Against Promoters

Picnic-goers display bodies, unusual talents, persistence

'naked. drunk people everywhere'

Willie Nelson's picnic-a smash

E Pluribus Willie

Willie on a Federal Reserve Note

Nelson Picnic Brings Different Musical Elements Together

HOLLYWOOD — This year's Willie Nelson 4th of July picnic was streamlined in production and presentation; narrowed to one day as opposed to three last year, and located on a privately-owned farm in Liberty Hill, some thirty miles northeast of Austin. The local populace expressed curiosity at the mix of lifestyles represented by the thousands of people who showed up to take part in a festival of high-energy music. No hostility was evident.

The music, an amalgamation of styles, including spiritual hymns, bluegrass, blues, country and western and rock and roll was presented by a variety of versatile artists. The performers and their audiences represent a progressive force in music. The blending of indigenous influences into contemporary sounds impossible to classify in any sense, except creative and dynamic, was the key to the affair.

The reason for the mass appeal is that people continually look for something new in music as their aesthetic senses evolve (both as performers and listeners) and they have found it in Texas. It's not that Texas is the sole progenitor of the new influence but at this point it seems to be most ready for performers who have versatility and ability to incorporate diverse musical forces. The Willie Nelson picnic highlighted the desire of artists to play what they like without stagnating within the conceptual boundaries which have, in the past, inhibited country artists who wanted to rock, or rock artists who wanted to pick. Almost any performer, regardless of his personal origins, will agree that Texas audiences are among the most receptive to music which has not been done before, and to that which has been done before but is now being done differently and/or better. The same performers will also testify that a Texas audience will boo an act off stage if it does poorly.

The open-mindedness, on both the audiences' and artists' parts, therefore, explains why rednecks and long-hairs, traditionalists, kids and adults alike can

sit together in an open field and be as receptive to the Pointer Sisters as to David Allen Coe or local resident Doug Sahm, and accept the mellow Rita Coolidge as

"THE RED-HEADED STRANGER" — Willie Nelson (center), played two sets with his own band as well as sitting in with several other performers during their sets. Pictured above are (l to r) Rex Ludwick on drums, Bobby (B.J.) Jones on guitar, Willie, Bobby Burns on keyboard, harmonica picker Mickey Raphael cooks behind bassist Bea Spears, and Jody Payne on lead guitar and backup vocals; when not backing Willie, these versatile lone star musicians' gig as "Too Hot For Snakes" throughout Texas. Not shown are pianist Bobbie Nelson, Willie's sister, and main drummer Paul English.

John Sebastian was a surprise guest; he ambled to the mike and said: 'I'm not really a member of this particular offshot . . . but I'm a second cousin from New York." After finishing three tunes with Too Hot For Snakes and KGBS progressive country disk jockey Jimmy Rabbitt on vocals, John knew he was definitely a part of the festival's spirit.

David Allen Coe waited nearly two hours to go on as the power was being restored; a late-afternoon shower stopped the show for awhile, cooling off the thousands of folks on hand but turning the dry pastureland to mud. Coe elicits sounds from his Gibson hollow-body that guarantee he will be creating for years to come.

Billy Swan and Kris Kristofferson (with Rita Coolidge and Donny Fritts) played for close to an hour and a half in their early-morning set before joining Willie and his band and family in an acapella "Amazing Grace" sung to the just-rising sun; a fitting close to an overall successful and rewarding 18 and a half hour experience.

well as the high-energy sound of the Charlie Daniels' Band, without complaining that a given artist is "too rock-oriented" or "too country-oriented." It doesn't matter anymore; the only label that fits is music.

There was a time when country performers trying to go pop thought it necessary to divest themselves of their country accents and musical roots; there was a time when rock and roll was dismissed as insular and inaccessible. Those days are gone, and performers of all persuasions are proud of their musical roots without being blind to the validity of other musical roots.

This is not to say that the contemporary progressive country movement is evolving into a formatted sound; on the contrary, it is essentially a matter of versatility. When any performer or artist is able to play several instruments, which may range from mandolin and dobro to drums and electric guitar, is able to play them well, and is able to use those diverse instruments in a set of songs ranging from the purest bluegrass to quality rock and roll, we see progression. It is inevitable that a well-rounded artist will be well received by a well-rounded audience; it is equally inevitable that an artist who creates limits for him/herself is not going to progress. An open mind leads to versatility.

The progressive movement in country music offers something for everybody and makes no attempt to deny traditional country (or any other) influences. Young people are listening to Bob Wills and Hank Williams today with as much, if not more, respect for their music and legend as when they were alive. But they are also listening to Willie Nelson, Ray Wiley Hubbard, Waylon Jennings, Jerry Jeff Walker, Tompall Glaser and others. The Willie Nelson picnic then does not stand as an isolated event in music; it stands as a statement of the past, present, and future of music that emanates from a love of the country, a love of simplicity without banality, and an honest look at life, love, and their inherently dynamic complexities.

The Willie Charisma

Who is this Willie Nelson and why is he hosting those giant music festivals?
By Mike Rhyner.

Buddy

The Original Texas Music Magazine
June, 1975   Vol. II, No. 12

Willie Nelson struggles to escape from an overzealous fan. Photo by Richard Pruitt.

What is this Willie Nelson charisma that has caused the redneck to make peace with the hippie? That can get the cowboy to sit in the dust and share a beer and a joint with a longhair? That can made an outdoor festival in Texas in July the nation's largest annual music event?

I'm afraid I can't answer that question. You have to experience for yourself the excitement of the Willie Nelson performance. The energy of the crowd, generated by the man with the gut-string guitar with a hole worn right through the top of it from years of hard pickin'.

Willie himself doesn't understand it. He just rolls with the punches, although it does give him a few anxious moments. Like a few weekends ago at an outdoor concert in Dallas when a young lady, sans shirt, was hoisted above the heads of the crowd and demanded a kiss from Willie. When he obliged she grabbed his guitar strap and wouldn't let go. Rather than be pulled off the 10-foot tall stage, Willie and some stagehands pulled her up and escorted her down the back steps. After regaining his composure, Willie returned to sing for a few more hours.

Willie's nationally famous outdoor country music spectacular, the Willie Nelson Third Annual Forth of July Picnic, will happen this year at Liberty Hill, Texas, about 30 miles north of Austin on a green country slope where the South Gabriel River winds into the Texas hill country.

The site is more accessible than the site of the historic 1st Annual Picnic near Dripping Springs and is covered with trees, two ponds and the winding fork of the San Gabriel River.

Appearing this year with Willie and his Family are the Pointer Sisters, the Charlie Daniels Band, Kris Kristofferson and Rita Coolidge, Billy Swan, Donnie Fritts, Doug Sahm, Billy C., Milton Carroll, Alex Harvey, Delbert McClinton, Johnny Bush, Floyd Tillman, and like all Willie Nelson performances, especially the Picnic, there will probably be a few artists appear unannounced. Leon Russell was onstage at sunup at Dripping Springs singing gospel songs to the early arrivers and last year John Sebastian and David Carradine spent the Forth in front of Texas Picnic freaks.

The State Of Texas

House Of Representatives
Certificate Of Citation

Pursuant to the motion of

Representative John Bryant

The House Of Representatives extends
sincere congratulations and directs the presentation
of this Certificate Of Citation to

WILLIE NELSON

a legendary exponent of the Texas brand of country music and member of
the prestigious Nashville Songwriters Hall of Fame, for his innumerable
musical achievements and the great pleasure he has brought to people
through his music and for his production of "Willie Nelson's Third Annual
4th of July Picnic," a famed outdoor music festival to be held this year in
Liberty Hill, Texas.

_____
Speaker of the House of Representatives

_____
Chief Clerk of the House of Representatives

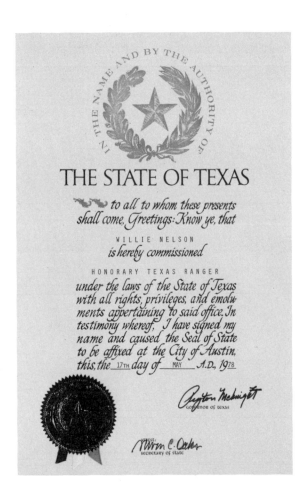

IN THE NAME AND BY THE AUTHORITY OF

THE STATE OF TEXAS

to all to whom these presents
shall come, Greetings: Know ye, that

WILLIE NELSON
is hereby commissioned

HONORARY TEXAS RANGER

under the laws of the State of Texas
with all rights, privileges, and emolu-
ments appertaining to said office. In
testimony whereof, I have signed my
name and caused the Seal of State
to be affixed at the City of Austin,
this, the 17TH day of MAY A.D., 1978

_____
GOVERNOR OF TEXAS

ATTEST:
_____
SECRETARY OF STATE

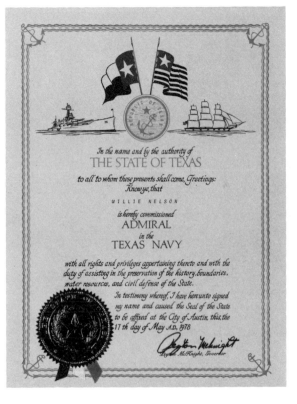

In the name and by the authority of
THE STATE OF TEXAS

to all to whom these presents shall come, Greetings:
Know ye, that

WILLIE NELSON

is hereby commissioned
ADMIRAL
in the
TEXAS NAVY

with all rights and privileges appertaining thereto and with the
duty of assisting in the preservation of the history, boundaries,
water resources, and civil defense of the State.

In testimony whereof, I have hereunto signed
my name and caused the Seal of the State
to be affixed at the City of Austin, this, the
17th day of May A.D. 1978

_____
Peyton McKnight, Governor

SENATE RESOLUTION

WHEREAS, The Senate is today honored with a visit from a great Texan whose music is loved by millions of Americans; and

WHEREAS, Mr. Willie Nelson was born at Abbott, Texas, in 1933, was brought up in Abbott by his grandparents, and after high school he enlisted in the Air Force; and

WHEREAS, His career as a musical performer began when, at the age of 10, he played the rhythm guitar in a Bohemian polka band in the town of West, Texas; and

WHEREAS, During most of the 1950's, Willie supported his family by selling vacuum cleaners, encyclopedias, and Bibles, by making saddles, or by working as a radio disc jockey, and then would spend his evenings writing and performing his songs; and

WHEREAS, He was the promoter for many North Central Texas appearances of the late, great Bob Wills and his Texas Playboys in the middle 1950's; and

WHEREAS, In 1960, Willie and his family moved to Nashville, Tennessee, then considered to be the headquarters for American country and western music, and the next year, Mr. Faron Young's recording of Willie's "Hello Walls" was the No. 1 song in the nation for 12 consecutive weeks; and

WHEREAS, Since then, Willie has recorded 25 record albums and has written hundreds of songs, including such American standards as "Funny How Time Slips Away," "Crazy," "The Night Life," "Pretty Paper," "The Party's Over," "Good Hearted Woman," and "Pretend I Never Happened"; and

WHEREAS, In 1970, he returned to his native Texas and since then has lived in or around Austin; and

WHEREAS, He was elected and inducted into the prestigious Nashville Songwriters Hall of Fame in 1973; and

WHEREAS, Since his return to Texas five years ago, Willie Nelson has become a folk hero to a whole new generation of music lovers, and as a result of the inspiration and encouragement he has provided to numerous young musicians, Austin is now nationally recognized for its music, and the music industry has become a major part of Austin's culture and economy; and

WHEREAS, This year, "Willie Nelson's Third Annual 4th of July Picnic," a day-long outdoor music concert, will be held in Liberty Hill, Texas; now, therefore, be it

RESOLVED, That the Senate of the 64th Legislature of the State of Texas hereby extend to Willie Nelson its appreciation for the enjoyment he and his music have brought to all Texans in the past, and its congratulations for his professional success and for the deserved high esteem in which he is held by millions of Americans; and, be it further

RESOLVED, That the date of July 4, 1975, in conjunction with "Willie Nelson's Third Annual 4th of July Picnic," be declared Willie Nelson Day in Texas in honor of this great Texan, and that a copy of this Resolution be prepared for this distinguished musician as a token of esteem from the Senate of Texas.

		Clower
		Doggett
		McKnight
Adams	Harrington	Moore
Aikin	Harris	Ogg
Andujar	Jones	Patman
Braecklein	Kothmann	Santiesteban
Brooks	Lombardino	Schwartz
Creighton	Longoria	Sherman
Farabee	Mauzy	Snelson
Gammage	McKinnon	Traeger
Hance	Meier	Williams
	Mengden	

Hobby, President of the Senate

WP Hobby
President of the Senate

I hereby certify that the above Resolution was adopted by the Senate on May 30, 1975.

Charles Schnabel
Secretary of the Senate

Tell 'em Willie's here, but sold out

HOUSTON CHRONICLE   Friday, April 4, 1975

Willie Nelson's Audience Begs for More and Gets It

Dallas Times Herald
June 22, 1975

Willie Nelson's giant reach

From a date with the Symphony to his annual 4th of July picnic

WILLIE NELSON and his favorite guitar, worn through just below the strings from his constant picking, will play the Dallas Symphony Orchestra's Summertop series and host his 3rd annual 4th of July picnic all in a week's time.

By KIM MARTIN
Entertainment Writer

Willie Nelson packs one powerful punch in Texas music. His fans are young; his fans are old. They're wild-eyed and mild mannered, homespun and elite. Willie reaches out his big musical hand across the giant spectrum of humanity and offers them all something spirited, something tangible, something Texan to reach for.

Within a scant week's time, Willie will be reaching out to two opposing ends of musical interest. Next Friday he takes his place on the Dallas Symphony Orchestra's Summertop bill at the big tent on NorthPark's parking lot. Then he will high-tail his way down to the hill country to host his third annual 4th of July picnic, this year at Liberty Hill.

THERE IS ALREADY speculation about just what Willie will wear for his DSO performance, and even symphony officials don't know yet what to expect. He may drag the old tux out of mothballs for his "formal" appearance. Or, more likely, he will show up in his traditional Willie uniform—faded blue jeans, T-shirt and those now-famous sneakers.

But in blue jeans or tux, the music will be the same—straight, pure Willie Nelson progressive Texas music, written as only he can write it.

It may not sound quite the same as it usually does, though. Special orchestral arrangements of Willie's songs like "Bloody Mary Morning," "Whiskey River" and "Shotgun Willie" have been prepared for the DSO engagement.

January Sound Studios' Chuck Mandernack — whose own musical acumen stretches easily from serious symphonic work to the free-wheeling Texas sound — has put together the arrangements, blending the two musical forces into one exceptional sound, showcasing the finest points of each.

The Summertop evening begins at 8:45 p.m. with the symphony taking the stage, playing Dallasound arrangements like "Overture to Rock" and the Aaron Copland favorite, "Billy the Kid Suite."

After intermission, the orchestra members will resume their places onstage, this time with Willie and Family in tow. They will perform the combined numbers together, before the King of Red Neck Rock takes over the stage by himself completely, playing until he gets tired of playing. That usually means a musical marathon running nonstop for at least a couple of hours.

DSO OPERATIONS manager Russel Gloyd thinks the crowd will prove to be an interesting one. About one-third of the audience will be series ticketholders. Another third, he says, will be the persons that know and love Willie who have rarely if ever been exposed to a symphonic orchestra. The rest will be just the opposite — persons attending Summertop to see the symphony, who may never have experienced a Willie Nelson show before.

Why is the DSO being paired with a progressive Texas act?

"To represent a total musical picture for the entire series," said Gloyd, "we wanted the finest performers in each particular field." Yep, for Texas music that would be Willie alright.

The Summertop series will present a variety of artists over the next several weeks, including Sarah Vaughan the night after Willie, plus Chet Atkins, Victor Borge, two generations of Brubeck and Roger Williams, all in July.

Summertop is a cabaret-styled set up in a huge tent, with tables toward the front and general admission seating at the back. Beverages, including soft drinks, beer and wine will be served, and each table has cheese and snacks.

The symphony will play through a custom-designed Jaffe Acoustics sound system, and a special air-circulation system has been installed.

Tickets, priced from $3.50 to $7, are available at the NorthPark Ticket Center, the Music Hall at Fair Park, the State Fair Box Office and Titche's Downtown.

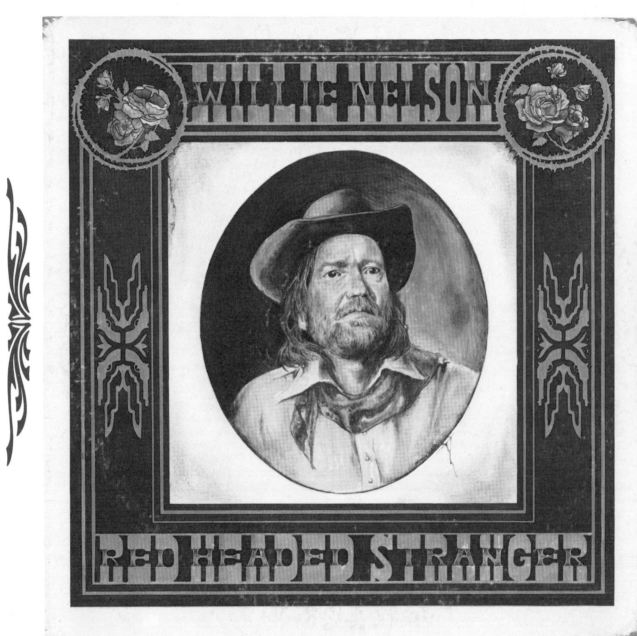

MATTHEW, MARK, LUKE, AND WILLIE

Willie Nelson's latest album is more than good country music;
it's almost gospel.

Country music, if you believe all the critics who have misread a recent movie called *Nashville*, is made up entirely of smarmy concoctions of drink, divorce, Fundamentalism, and other cheap, unchic subjects. Country musicians, if one subscribes to *Nashville*'s credo, are perhaps one generation removed from cave dwellers. Their primitive musical instincts reveal themselves in cretinous tunes that parallel their wretched lives lived out in an alcoholic daze. Their existence is bounded by '52 Buicks, trailer parks, and divorce court.

Country music sometimes may reflect such a life—but it is much, much more in the hands of its few truly gifted songwriters. The best of them—and this will come as no surprise to Texans—is a man named Willie Nelson who has recently recorded an album so remarkable that it calls for a redefinition of the term "country music." The difference between Nelson's *Red Headed Stranger* and any other current C&W album, and especially what passes for a soundtrack for *Nashville*, is astounding. What Nelson has done is simply unclassifiable; it is the only record I have ever heard that strikes me as otherworldly. *Red Headed Stranger* conjures up such strange emotions and works on so many levels that listening to it becomes totally obsessing. The world that Nelson has created is so seductive that you want to linger there indefinitely.

Basically, *Stranger* is a morality play that has a lot to do with honor and integrity and revenge and style and good and evil and God and the universe. The story line, on the surface, is this: the Stranger's woman leaves him for another man, he tracks them down and kills them; in tormented mourning he

rides aimlessly and wildly and shoots a woman who tries to steal the "dancing bay pony" that had belonged to his woman; along the way he undergoes a massive catharsis, an emotional death and rebirth and eventual salvation and acceptance of life through another woman he meets. Together, they build a new life. A simple plot, to be sure, but Nelson's telling of it is extraordinary. The usual music industry term "concept album" is inadequate. *Stranger* is more a revival of the oral tradition, of the storyteller who preserves and passes on the beliefs and teachings of a tribe or group.

Nelson has given hints for years that he was capable of assuming such a role. Of all contemporary songwriters, he has most effectively observed and interpreted life around him. The master of despair, the poet of honky tonks, the chronicler of personal apocalypse—he has been called all of these and they are all accurate. After all, any man who could write a touching song about a man strangling his lover, another in which a despairing solitary man talks to the walls, and yet another with the remarkable title "Darkness on the Face of the Earth" is a man who walks close to the edge. That in itself is not unusual in country songwriters. Since the days of Jimmie Rodgers and the Carter Family right up through Hank Williams to Merle Haggard the music has dealt with the life the songwriters knew and they depicted it in realistic terms. There has been little escapism in country lyrics and almost no fantasy. It's been largely grim music that dealt with life's central problems: problems with the job down at the plant, marital difficulties, hopelessly transparent love affairs, sor-

did one-night stands, and endless troubles with the bottle.

Musicians like Nelson have refined these themes. Country music, as it broadened its horizons and pushed against its boundaries, has begun to attract a new generation of listeners and a cluster of young songwriters. Nelson remains the doyen of the new school, as he proved with his last album. *Phases and Stages* was a compassionate account of the dissolution of a marriage, which gave extremely sensitive male and female viewpoints. It, again, was labeled a "concept album" but I would call it a musical documentary.

I notice with interest that a single release off *Stranger*, "Blue Eyes Crying In the Rain," has made a small noise for itself on the country charts. What's astonishing is that Nelson, the master storyteller, did not write that song (Fred Rose of Nashville did); nor did he write much of the material on *Stranger*. He anthologized songs that span decades of American musical history and amazingly, once they were put together, they formed an unbroken tale. The effect is the same as if the entire album had been written at one sitting.

Nelson's transitional device is his own "Time of the Preacher Theme," with variations. The album opens with his weary, voice-of-a-prophet tale: "It was a time of the Preacher, when the story began, of the choice of a lady, and the love of a man. How he loved her so dearly, he went out of his mind, when she left him for someone, that she'd left behind."* Timeless elements, these, and a classic basis for tragedy: romantic triangle, wronged lover, moral teachings, and inevitable revenge. The imagery, like the music instrumentation, is sparse and bleak: the wronged man "cried like a baby and screamed like a panther in the middle of the night. It was a time of the Preacher, in the year of '01. Now the preachin' is over, and the lesson's begun."*

The next song—or movement or chapter or whatever these installments should be called—is about mourning and garment tearing and smearing of ashes on one's forehead and the pro-

foundest grief over the loss. "I couldn't believe it was true, O Lord," sings the Stranger. If you're of the opinion that Nelson's morality play parallels the Book of Genesis, the retelling of it in frontier terms yields a surprise. Instead of reconciling himself to being cast out, the Stranger burns with an inner fire and could not possibly refrain from tracking down and shooting the woman and the viper who ended his happiness.

The Stranger "could not forgive her, though he tried and he tried. And the halls of his memory still echoed her lies. He cried like a baby and screamed like a panther in the middle of the night. And he saddled his pony and went for a ride. It was a time of the Preacher in the year of '01. Now the lesson is over, and the killin's begun."* Revenge is his. But after he slays the woman and the other man, revenge is not enough. With his "eyes like the thunder," the Stranger rides hell-bent to nowhere, like some terrifying Death Angel on his black stallion. He senses, in the throes of bitter remorse, that he can regain innocence lost, that he can again know the happiness that was his. He does not know how but, eventually, through resisting a false savior (a temptress whom he shoots), he comes to recognize and finally accept his fate. Side one ends with "Just As I Am," the timeless and haunting gospel of total surrender to God.

On side two, he finds his reward in the form of a woman who will accept him: "With no place to hide, I looked in your eyes. And I found myself in you. I looked to the stars, tried all of the bars. And I've nearly gone up in smoke. Now my hand's on the wheel of something that's real. And I feel like I'm going home."† Closing the tale is a pastoral guitar instrumental, "Bandera," that suggests a vision of a second Eden.

Listeners with a sense of whimsy may want to file this record, this Willie Nelson Version, next to the King James or the Revised Standard Version.

* Copyright 1975 by Willie Nelson Music, Inc. (BMI).
† "Hands On the Wheel," by Bill Collery. Copyright 1975 by Nunn Publishing Company (BMI).

In 1975 Willie recorded on Columbia "Blue Eyes Crying in the Rain," which eventually won a grammy. His band consisted of Bobbie Nelson on piano, Paul English on drums, Dan "Bee" Spears on bass, Jody Payne on guitar, and Mickey Raphael on harmonica.

Paul   Bee   Bobbie

Jody   Mickey   Chris   Rex

In 1976 Rex Ludwig joined the band as a second drummer.
And in 1977 bass player Chris Ethridge joined the band.
Willie had undoubtedly the hottest band in country music.

AUSTIN NOTES

July, 1977

Willie and Waylon open The Austin Opry House

Sound in Your Mind

Well, I've been feelin' a little bad,
'Cause I've been feelin' a little better without you.
It's a little like rain,
But it's a lot like a sunny day.

And it's hard to explain,
But the sound of your name don't make music anymore.
It's more of a sound
Of a love that I lost one day.

Well, it's a little too late
To start thinkin' about startin' all over.
I'd rather stay where I am.
I can't take another slam in the mind.

And I been feelin' a little bad,
'Cause I been feelin' a little better without you.
But remember my love
Is the sound that you hear in your mind.

And I been runnin' around
Even laughing at half of the mem'ries
And you're not hard to remember.
I just have to think of your name.

And I been feelin' a little bad,
'Cause I been feelin' a little better without you.
But remember my love
Is the sound that you hear in your mind.

"I've been many things in my life.
I've sold encyclopedias, vacuum cleaners, and Bibles.
I even trimmed trees and made saddles."

 Columbia

 **WILLIE NELSON**

Representation:
MARK ROTHBAUM

1979 finds Willie with four platinum albums: "Red Headed Stranger," "The Outlaws," "Waylon and Willie," and "Stardust." This same year Willie was awarded Country Music Association's top honor, Entertainer of the Year.

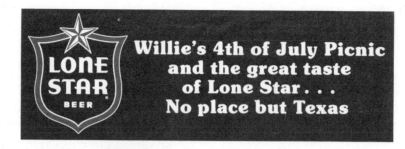

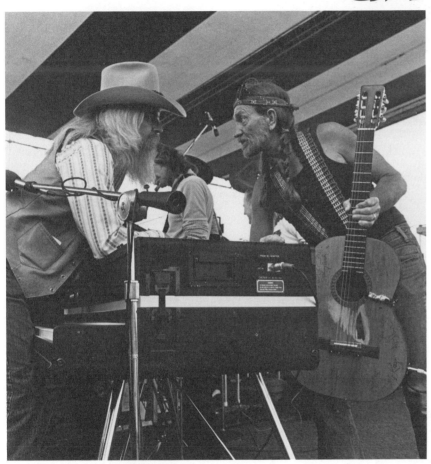

Leon Russell and Willie
at 1979 picnic

Ernest Tubb and Willie
singing "Waltz across Texas"

Snake

Poody

Schroder

Beast

David

Cooper

Steve

Mr. Willie Nelson

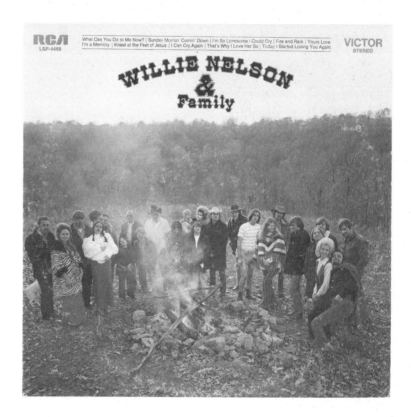

WILLIE

Hello there. Let's start this issue off with congratulations to the winner of the "What Willie's Music Has Meant to My Life" contest, MARY SOILEAU of Alexandria, Louisiana. Mary has promised to write about her trip to Tahoe so it can be shared by the rest of us. Her winning entry follows below

"WHAT WILLIE'S MUSIC HAS MEANT TO MY LIFE"

Willie's music changed my life. I heard Willie sing and I had to see him. After that concert I couldn't wait for stores to open so I could buy Willie's records. For the first time in my life I joined a fan club so I'd know where and when Willie was singing. We began planning week-ends according to where Willie was singing, although I'm in poor health and limited in my activities.

An extra of Willie's music is the people you meet through mutual love for Willie. I've met people throughout Louisiana, in Texas, even have a pen-pal in Florida because we love Willie and his music. Willie's music brings out special feelings in people. I think it's because his music tells of people the way we really are and lets us know we all belong to the same family.

Willie's concerts are special but one I'd like to share. Willie did a concert in my home town. I had to have up front tickets. The day before tickets went on sale I went to check. People were already in line. My heart began breaking. I knew it was impossible for me to stay outdoors all night. It got colder, I began making my way to the car. Suddenly a stranger called to me. She asked why I was leaving. I mentioned one problem and without pause she replied, "I'll get your tickets and you'll have as good a seat as mine." I had a front row seat.

That's what Willie's music means to people and to me.

Thank you Willie, your devoted fan,
MARY (MRS. RUDIE R.) SOILEAU
ALEXANDRIA, LOUISIANA

Willie at the White House
April 25, 1978

The children

Lana, Billy, and Susie

Willie, Connie, Paula Carleene, and Amy

The grandchildren

Nelson Ray

Rebecca

Bryan

Rachel

Martha

Goin' Home

The closer I get to my home, Lord, the more I want to be there.
There'll be a gathering of loved ones and friends, and you know I want to be there.
There'll be a mixture of tear drops and flowers,
Crying and talking for hours
About how wild that I was
And if I'd listened to them, I wouldn't be there.

Well there's old Charlie Tolk, they threw away the mold when they made him.
And Jimmy McKline, looks like the wines finally laid him.
And Billy McGray, I could beat any day in a card game.
And Bessy McNeil, but her tears are real, I can see pain.
There's a mixture of tear drops and flowers,
Crying and talking for hours
About how wild that I was,
And if I'd listened to them, I wouldn't be there.

Lord, thanks for the ride, I got a feeling inside that I know you,
And if you see your way, you're welcome to stay 'cause I'm gonna need you.
There's a mixture of tear drops and flowers,
Crying and talking for hours
About how wild that I was
And if I'd listened to them, I wouldn't be there.

Love, Lana

Willie Nelson Catalog

"Ain't It Funny How Wine Sips Away?"
publisher: Tree Publishing Co., Inc.
co-writer: Sheb Wooley, one-half share
clearance: 4-30-68

"And So Will You My Love"
publisher: Tree Publishing Co., Inc.
clearance: 10-31-65

"Any Old Arms Won't Do"
publisher: Tree Publishing Co., Inc.
co-writer: Hank Cochran, one-half share
clearance: 6-30-64

"Are You Ever Coming Home?" AKA
"Darling Are You Ever Coming Home?"
publisher: Tree Publishing Co., Inc.
co-writer: Hank Cochran, one-half share
clearance: 6-30-64

"Are You Sure?"
publisher: Tree Publishing Co., Inc.
co-writer: Bobby Emmons, one-half share
clearance: 2-28-62

"Ashamed"
publisher: Tree Publishing Co., Inc.
clearance: 4-30-68

"Bloody Mary Morning"
publisher: Willie Nelson Music, Inc.
clearance: 7-31-70

"Both Ends of the Candle"
publisher: Tree Publishing Co., Inc.
clearance: 5-31-64

"Buddy"
publisher: Tree Publishing Co., Inc.
clearance: 6-30-65

"Chain of Love"
publisher: Tree Publishing Co., Inc.
clearance: 1-10-62

"Cold Empty Space"
publisher: Tree Publishing Co., Inc.
co-writer: James C. Day, one-half share
clearance: 7-31-68

"Congratulations"
publisher: Tree Publishing Co., Inc.
clearance: 4-15-61

"Country Willie"
publisher: Tree Publishing Co., Inc.
clearance: 12-1-61

"Crazy"
publisher: Tree Publishing Co., Inc.
clearance: 12-1-61

"Crying in the Heart"
publisher: Glad Music Company
co-writer: Hank Craig, one-quarter share
clearance: 2-29-60

"Cry Softly Darling"
publisher: Tree Pub shing Co., Inc.
co-writer: Harlan Howard, one-half share
clearance: 3-31-62

"Darkness on the Face of the Earth"
publisher: Tree Publishing Co., Inc.
clearance: 12-1-61

"December Day"
publisher: Tree Publishing Co., Inc.
clearance: 3-31-68

"Devil in a Sleepin' Bag"
publisher: Willie Nelson Music, Inc.
clearance: 8-7-73

"Did I Ever Love You?"
publisher: Tree Publishing Co., Inc.
clearance: 4-30-66

"Don't Say Love or Nothing"
publisher: Tree Publishing Co., Inc.
clearance: 5-31-67

"Down at the Corner Beer Joint"
publisher: Willie Nelson Music, Inc.
clearance: 2-28-73

"End of Understanding, The"
publisher: Tree Publishing Co., Inc.
clearance: 5-31-62

"Everybody's Baby"
publisher: Tree Publishing Co., Inc.
clearance: 12-31-64

"Everything but You"
publisher: Tree Publishing Co., Inc.
co-writer: Hank Cochran, one-half share
clearance: 5-31-62

"Face of a Fighter"
publisher: Tree Publishing Co., Inc.
clearance: 5-31-62

"Following Me Around"
publisher: Willie Nelson Music, Inc.
clearance: 10-26-70

"Funny" AKA "Funny How Time Slips Away"
publisher: Tree Publishing Co., Inc.
clearance: 9-30-64

"Ghost, The"
publisher: Tree Publishing Co., Inc.
clearance: 2-28-62

"Go Away"
publisher: Tree Publishing Co., Inc.
clearance: 12-1-61

"Goin' Home"
publisher: Willie Nelson Music, Inc.
clearance: 9-24-71

"Good Hearted Woman, A"
publishers: Baron Music, one-half share
Willie Nelson Music, Inc., one-half share
co-writer: Waylon Jennings, one-half share
clearance: 11-19-71

"Good Times"
publisher: Tree Publishing Co., Inc.
clearance: 6-30-68

"Half a Man"
publisher: Tree Publishing Co., Inc.
clearance: 5-31-62

"Happiness Lives Next Door"
publisher: Tree Publishing Co., Inc.
clearance: 5-31-62

"Healing Hands of Time"
publisher: Tree Publishing Co., Inc.
clearance: 11-30-64

"Heaven and Hell"
publisher: Willie Nelson Music, Inc.
clearance: 2-25-74

"Hello Darling"
publisher: Tree Publishing Co., Inc.
co-writer: Betty Logan, one-half share
clearance: 8-31-61

"Hello Fool"
publisher: Tree Publishing Co., Inc.
co-writer: Jim Coleman, one-half share
clearance: 8-31-61

"Hello Wall Number 2"
publisher: Tree Publishing Co., Inc.
co-writer: Sheb Wooley, one-half share
clearance: 4-30-63

"Hello Walls"
publisher: Tree Publishing Co., Inc.
clearance: 4-15-61

"He's Not for You"
publisher: Tree Publishing Co., Inc.
clearance: 5-31-63

"Hold Me Tighter"
publisher: Tree Publishing Co., Inc.
clearance: 1-31-63

"Homecoming in Heaven"
publisher: Glad Music Company
co-writers: Claude Gray, one-quarter share
Walter M. Breeland, one-quarter share
Paul F. Buskirk, one-quarter share
clearance: 10-31-60

"Home Is Where You're Happy"
publisher: Tree Publishing Co., Inc.
clearance: 8-31-66

"Home Motel"
publisher: Tree Publishing Co., Inc.
clearance: 1-31-63

"How Does It Feel?"
publisher: Tree Publishing Co., Inc.
co-writer: Hank Cochran, one-half share
clearance: 5-31-64

"How Long Is Forever?"
publisher: Tree Publishing Co., Inc.
clearance: 12-1-61

"I Can Cry Again"
publisher: Willie Nelson Music, Inc.
clearance: 9-24-71

"I Can Still Reach Yesterday"
publisher: Tree Publishing Co., Inc.
clearance: 6-30-66

"I Can't Find the Time"
publisher: Tree Publishing Co., Inc.
co-writer: Hank Cochran, one-half share
clearance: 8-31-61

"I Didn't Sleep a Wink"
publisher: Tree Publishing Co., Inc.
co-writer: Jimmy Day, one-half share
clearance: 12-1-61

"I Don't Feel Anything"
publisher: Tree Publishing Co., Inc.
clearance: 5-31-67

"I Don't Understand"
clearance: 1-1-63

"I'd Rather You Didn't Love Me"
publisher: Glad Music Company
co-writers: Claude Gray, one-quarter share
Walter M. Breeland, one-quarter share
clearance: 6-30-62

"I Feel Sorry for Him"
publisher: Tree Publishing Co., Inc.
clearance: 8-31-62

"If You Could Only See"
publisher: Willie Nelson Music, Inc.
clearance: 10-22-74

"If You Really Loved Me"
publisher: Willie Nelson Music, Inc.
clearance: 6-12-72

"I Gotta Get Drunk"
publisher: Tree Publishing Co., Inc.
clearance: 6-30-63

"I Just Can't Let You Say Goodbye"
publisher: Tree Publishing Co., Inc.
clearance: 10-31-65

"I Just Don't Understand"
publisher: Tree Publishing Co., Inc.
clearance: 9-30-62

"I Just Stopped By"
publisher: Tree Publishing Co., Inc.
clearance: 9-30-62

"I Let My Mind Wander"
publisher: Tree Publishing Co., Inc.
clearance: 8-31-66

"I'll Stay Around"
publisher: Tree Publishing Co., Inc.
co-writer: Hank Cochran, one-half share
clearance: 5-31-62

"I'm a Memory"
publisher: Willie Nelson Music, Inc.
clearance: 5-10-71

"I'm Falling in Love Again"
publisher: Willie Nelson Music, Inc.
clearance: 2-28-73

"I'm So Ashamed"
publisher: Tree Publishing Co., Inc.
clearance: 5-31-64

"I'm Still Not Over You"
publisher: Tree Publishing Co., Inc.
clearance: 5-31-66

"I Never Cared for You"
publisher: Tree Publishing Co., Inc.
clearance: 5-31-64

"In God's Eyes"
publisher: Tree Publishing Co., Inc.
clearance: 12-1-61

"I Should Have Kissed Her More"
publisher: Tree Publishing Co., Inc.
co-writers: Hank Cochran, one-third share
Fred F. Carter, Jr., one-third share
clearance: 1-31-65

"I Still Can't Believe You're Gone"
publisher: Willie Nelson Music, Inc.
clearance: 2-25-74

"It Could Be Said That Way"
publisher: Willie Nelson Music, Inc.
clearance: 7-31-70

"It Should Be Easier Now"
publisher: Tree Publishing Co., Inc.
clearance: 12-31-63

"It's Not for Me to Understand"
publisher: Tree Publishing Co., Inc.
clearance: 6-30-63

"It's Not Supposed to Be That Way"
publisher: Willie Nelson Music, Inc.
clearance: 5-14-74

"I've Got a Wonderful Future Behind Me"
publisher: Glad Music Company
clearance: 12-10-73

"I've Just Destroyed the World I'm Living In"
publisher: Tree Publishing Co., Inc.
co-writer: Ray Price, one-half share
clearance: 3-31-62

"I've Seen All This World I Care to See"
publisher: Tree Publishing Co., Inc.
clearance: 5-31-64

"I Want a Girl"
publisher: Tree Publishing Co., Inc.
clearance: 8-31-61

"I Want to Be Alone"
publisher: Glad Music Company
co-writers: Walter M. Breeland, one-quarter share
Paul F. Buskirk, one-quarter share
clearance: 12-31-60

"I Write You Letters"
publisher: Tree Publishing Co., Inc.
co-writer: Harlan Howard, two-thirds share
clearance: 12-1-61

"Jimmy's Road"
publisher: Tree Publishing Co., Inc.
clearance: 9-30-68

"Just for the Moment"
publisher: Tree Publishing Co., Inc.
clearance: 3-31-64

"Kneel at the Feet of Jesus"
publisher: Tree Publishing Co., Inc.
clearance: 5-31-62

"Laying My Burdens Down"
publisher: Willie Nelson Music, Inc.
clearance: 10-26-70

"Leave Alone"
publisher: Glad Music Company
co-writers: Claude Gray, one-quarter share
Walter M. Breeland, one-quarter share
clearance: 6-30-60

"Let Me Be a Man"
publisher: Willie Nelson Music, Inc.
clearance: 9-24-71

"Let My Heart Be Broken"
publisher: Tree Publishing Co., Inc.
co-writer: Harlan Howard, one-half share
clearance: 8-31-61

"Little Things"
publisher: Tree Publishing Co., Inc.
co-writer: Shirley Nelson, one-half share
clearance: 2-29-68

"Local Memory, The"
publisher: Tree Publishing Co., Inc.
clearance: 12-31-63

"London"
publisher: Willie Nelson Music, Inc.
clearance: 6-12-72

"Lonely Little Mansion"
publisher: Tree Publishing Co., Inc.
clearance: 12-31-61

"Man with the Blues"
publisher: Glad Music Company
clearance: 9-30-64

"Me and Paul"
publisher: Willie Nelson Music, Inc.
clearance: 9-24-71

"Mean Old Greyhound Bus"
publisher: Tree Publishing Co., Inc.
co-writer: Hank Cochran, one-half share
clearance: 6-30-64

"Message, The"
publisher: Tree Publishing Co., Inc.
clearance: 8-31-66

"Misery Mansion"
publisher: Glad Music Company
co-writer: Hank Craig, one-quarter share
clearance: 4-30-60

"Moment Isn't Very Long, A"
publisher: Tree Publishing Co., Inc.
clearance: 8-31-61

"More than One Way to Cry"
publisher: Tree Publishing Co., Inc.
clearance: 7-31-65

"Mr. Record Man"
publisher: Tree Publishing Co., Inc.
clearance: 12-1-61

"My Kind of Girl"
publisher: Willie Nelson Music, Inc.
clearance: 6-12-72

"My Own Peculiar Way"
publisher: Tree Publishing Co., Inc.
clearance: 3-31-64

"My Party's Over"
publishers: Hills Music, one-half share
          Glad Music Company, one-half share
clearance: 6-30-60

"New Way to Cry, A"
publisher: Tree Publishing Co., Inc.
clearance: 12-1-61

"Night Life"
publisher: Reeny Rhythms, Inc.
co-writers: Paul Buskirk, one-quarter share
          Walter M. Breeland, one-quarter share
clearance: 5-31-62

"Night Life"
publishers: Glad Music Company, one-half share
          Tree Publishing Co., Inc., one-half share
co-writers: Paul F. Buskirk, one-quarter share
          Walter M. Breeland, one-quarter share
clearance: 5-31-62

"No Love Around"
publisher: Willie Nelson Music, Inc.
clearance: 2-28-73

"No Tomorrow in Sight"
publisher: Tree Publishing Co., Inc.
clearance: 10-3-61

"Once Alone"
publisher: Tree Publishing Co., Inc.
clearance: 2-28-62

"One Day at a Time"
publisher: Tree Publishing Co., Inc.
clearance: 3-31-65

"One in a Row"
publisher: Tree Publishing Co., Inc.
clearance: 8-31-66

"One Step Beyond"
publisher: Tree Publishing Co., Inc.
clearance: 12-1-61

"Opportunity to Cry"
publisher: Tree Publishing Co., Inc.
clearance: 6-30-63

"Our Chain of Love"
publisher: Tree Publishing Co., Inc.
clearance: 12-31-61

"Pages"
publisher: Tree Publishing Co., Inc.
co-writers: Lana Nelson, one-third share
          Shirley Nelson, one-third share
clearance: 2-29-68

"Part Where I Cry"
publisher: Tree Publishing Co., Inc.
clearance: 8-31-61

"Party's Over, The"
publishers: Heart of the Hills Publishing, one-half share
          Tree Publishing Co., Inc., one-half share
clearance: 12-31-67

"Permanently Lonely"
publisher: Tree Publishing Co., Inc.
clearance: 6-30-63

"Phases Stages Circles Cycles and Scenes"
publisher: Willie Nelson Music, Inc.
clearance: 2-28-73

"Pick Up the Tempo"
publisher: Willie Nelson Music, Inc.
clearance: 5-15-74

"Pretend I Never Happened"
publisher: Willie Nelson Music, Inc.
clearance: 2-28-73

"Pretty Paper"
publisher: Tree Publishing Co., Inc.
clearance: 1-31-63

"Pullamo"
publisher: Sophisticate Music, Inc.
co-writer: Steve Pulliam, one-half share
clearance: 3-49

"Pussy"
publisher: Bridgeport Music
co-writers: George Clinton, Jr., one-third share
          Eddie Hazel, one-third share
clearance: 7-24-73

"Rainy Day Blues"
publisher: Glad Music Company
clearance: 10-31-63

"Remember the Good Times"
publisher: Willie Nelson Music, Inc.
clearance: 9-24-71

"Ridge Top"
publisher: Tree Publishing Co., Inc.
clearance: 5-31-64

"Run Jody Run"
publisher: Willie Nelson Music, Inc.
clearance: 10-22-74

"Sad Songs and Waltzes"
publisher: Tree Publishing Co., Inc.
clearance: 8-31-64

"Save Your Tears"
publisher: Tree Publishing Co., Inc.
clearance: 12-1-61

"She Always Comes Back to Me"
publisher: Tree Publishing Co., Inc.
co-writer: Hank Cochran, one-half share
clearance: 3-31-64

"She Might Call"
publisher: Tree Publishing Co., Inc.
clearance: 1-31-63

"She's Not for You"
publisher: Tree Publishing Co., Inc.
clearance: 1-31-63

"She's Still Gone"
publisher: Tree Publishing Co., Inc.
co-writer: Shirley Nelson, one-half share
clearance: 6-30-68

"Shotgun Willie"
publisher: Willie Nelson Music, Inc.
clearance: 8-7-73

"Sister's Coming Home"
publisher: Willie Nelson Music, Inc.
clearance: 2-28-73

"Slow Down Old World"
publisher: Tree Publishing Co., Inc.
clearance: 12-31-67

"Some Other Time"
publisher: Tree Publishing Co., Inc.
clearance: 12-1-61

"Something to Think About"
publisher: Tree Publishing Co., Inc.
clearance: 8-31-66

"Sometimes She Lies"
publisher: Tree Publishing Co., Inc.
co-writer: Harlan Howard, one-half share
clearance: 1-31-63

"So Much to Do"
publisher: Tree Publishing Co., Inc.
clearance: 6-30-65

"Sorrow Tearing Me Apart"
publisher: Tree Publishing Co., Inc.
clearance: 7-31-65

"Storm Within My Heart, The"
publisher: Western Hills Music Corp.
clearance: 6-30-60

"Suffer in Silence"
publisher: Tree Publishing Co., Inc.
clearance: 8-31-62

"Summer of Roses"
publisher: Willie Nelson Music, Inc.
clearance: 9-24-71

"Take My Word"
publisher: Tree Publishing Co., Inc.
clearance: 8-31-62

"Talk to Me"
publisher: Tree Publishing Co., Inc.
clearance: 5-31-65

"That's What Children Are For"
publisher: Four Star Music Company, Inc.
clearance: 12-31-60

"That's Why I Love Her"
publisher: Willie Nelson Music, Inc.
clearance: 9-24-71

"There Is No Easy Way" AKA "There's a Way"
publisher: Tree Publishing Co., Inc.
clearance: 12-31-63

"There's a Way"
publisher: Tree Publishing Co., Inc.
clearance: 12-1-61

"There's Gonna Be Love in My House"
publisher: Tree Publishing Co., Inc.
clearance: 8-31-62

"There's No Tomorrow in Sight"
publisher: Tree Publishing Co., Inc.
clearance: 12-31-67

"These Are Difficult Times"
publisher: Willie Nelson Music, Inc.
clearance: 9-24-71

"They're All the Same"
publisher: Tree Publishing Co., Inc.
clearance: 1-31-66

"Things to Remember"
publisher: Tree Publishing Co., Inc.
clearance: 8-31-61

"Three Days"
publisher: Tree Publishing Co., Inc.
co-writer: Faron Young, one-half share
clearance: 8-31-61

"Today's Gonna Make a Wonderful Yesterday"
publisher: Tree Publishing Co., Inc.
clearance: 8-31-66

"To Make a Long Story Short" AKA "She's Gone"
publisher: Tree Publishing Co., Inc.
co-writer: Fred L. Foster, one-half share
clearance: 5-31-64

"Too Young to Settle Down"
publisher: Central Songs, Inc.
co-writer: Jack Rhodes, one-half share
clearance: 10-12-56

"Touch Me"
publisher: Tree Publishing Co., Inc.
clearance: 5-31-62

"Turn out the Lights" AKA "The Party's Over"
publisher: Glad Music Company
co-writer: Hank Craig, one-quarter share
clearance: 3-31-60

"Twice the Man"
publisher: Tree Publishing Co., Inc.
co-writers: Edwin Greines, one-quarter share
Maribeth Murry, one-quarter share
clearance: 10-8-70

"Two Different Roads"
publisher: Tree Publishing Co., Inc.
co-writers: Jan L. Curtchfield, one-third share
Hank Cochran, one-third share
clearance: 2-28-62

"Undo the Right"
publisher: Tree Publishing Co., Inc.
co-writer: Hank Cochran, one-half share
clearance: 12-1-61

"Waiting Time"
publisher: Tree Publishing Co., Inc.
clearance: 12-1-61

"Wake Me When It's Over"
publisher: Tree Publishing Co., Inc.
clearance: 9-30-62

"Walkin' "
publisher: Willie Nelson Music, Inc.
clearance: 5-15-74

"Wanted One Mother"
publisher: Tree Publishing Co., Inc.
co-writer: Harlan Howard, one-half share
clearance: 10-31-65

"What a Way to Live"
publisher: Glad Music Company
co-writer: Hank Craig, one-quarter share
clearance: 4-30-60

"What Can You Do to Me Now?"
publishers: Willie Nelson Music, Inc., one-half share
Twig Music Incorporated, one-half share
co-writer: Hank Cochran, one-half share
clearance: 12-8-70

"What Do You Think of Her Bow?"
publisher: Tree Publishing Co., Inc.
co-writer: Hank Cochran, one-half share
clearance: 9-30-61

"What Do You Want Me To Do?"
publisher: Willie Nelson Music, Inc.
clearance: 2-25-74

"What Right Have I?"
publisher: Pardner Publishing Company
clearance: (no date)

"When We Live Again"
publisher: Willie Nelson Music, Inc.
clearance: 10-26-70

"Where Do You Stand?"
publisher: Willie Nelson Music, Inc.
clearance: 10-26-70

"Where My House Lives"
publisher: Tree Publishing Co., Inc.
clearance: 12-1-61

"Where's the Show?"
publisher: Willie Nelson Music, Inc.
clearance: 9-24-71

"Who Do I Know in Dallas?"
publisher: Tree Publishing Co., Inc.
co-writer: Hank Cochran, one-half share
clearance: 4-30-68

"Who'll Buy My Memories?"
publisher: Glad Music Company
co-writer: Eddie Noack, one-half share
clearance: 6-30-63

"Why Are You Picking on Me?"
publisher: Tree Publishing Co., Inc.
clearance: 8-31-66

"Will You Remember?"
publisher: Tree Publishing Co., Inc.
clearance: 9-30-61

"Within Your Crowd"
publisher: Tree Publishing Co., Inc.
clearance: 1-31-63

"Wonderful Future"
Publisher: Glad Music Company
clearance: 12-1-61

"Words Don't Fit the Picture, The"
publisher: Willie Nelson Music, Inc.
clearance: 6-12-72

"Yesterday's Wine"
publisher: Willie Nelson Music, Inc.
clearance: 9-24-71

"You Dream About Me"
publisher: Tree Publishing Co., Inc.
clearance: 1-30-62

"You Left a Long Time Ago"
publisher: Tree Publishing Co., Inc.
clearance: 6-30-64

"You'll Always Have Someone"
publisher: Tree Publishing Co., Inc.
co-writer: Hank Cochran, one-half share
clearance: 6-30-64

"You Ought to Hear Me Cry"
publisher: Tree Publishing Co., Inc.
clearance: 5-31-67

"Your Country Boy"
publisher: Tree Publishing Co., Inc.
clearance: 7-31-64

"You Took My Happy Away"
publisher: Tree Publishing Co., Inc.
clearance: 6-30-63

"You Wouldn't Cross the Street"
publisher: Tree Publishing Co., Inc.
clearance: 8-31-62

 # Discography

Label	Number	Title
Liberty	LST-7239	" . . . and Then I Wrote"
Liberty	LST-7308	"Here's Willie Nelson"
Sunset	SNS-5138	"Hello Walls"
RCA	LSP-3418	"Country Willie—His Own Songs"
RCA	LSP-3528	"Country Favorites—Willie Nelson Style"
RCA	LSP-3659	"Country Music Concert" (Live at Panther Hall)
RCA	LSP-3748	"Make Way for Willie Nelson"
RCA	LSP-3858	"The Party's Over"
RCA	LSP-3937	"Texas in My Soul"
RCA	LSP-4057	"Good Times"
RCA	LSP-4111	"My Own Peculiar Way"
RCA	LSP-4294	"Both Sides Now"
RCA	LSP-4404	"Laying My Burdens Down"
RCA	LSP-4489	"Willie Nelson and Family"
RCA*	LSP-4568	"Yesterday's Wine"
RCA	LSP-4653	"The Words Don't Fit the Picture"
RCA	LSP-4760	"The Willie Way"
RCA-Camden	ACLI-0326	"Country Winners" (Reissued by Pickwick Records #ACL-0326)
RCA-Camden	ACLI-0705	"Spotlight on Willie Nelson" (Reissued by Pickwick Records #ACL-0705)
RCA*	APLI-1234	"What Can You Do to Me Now?"
RCA*	APLI-1321	"The Outlaws"
RCA-Camden	CAS-2444	"Columbus Stockade Blues" (Reissue of most of "Country Favorites" RCA-LSP-3528)
United Artists	LA086-F	"The Best of Willie Nelson" (Reissue of ". . . and Then I Wrote" Liberty LST-7239)
United Artists*	LA410-G	"Country Willie"
United Artists*	LA574-H2	"Texas Country"
Atlantic*	SD-7262	"Shotgun Willie"
Atlantic*	SD-7291	"Phases and Stages"
Columbia*	KC-33482	"Red Headed Stranger"
Columbia*	KC-34092	"The Sound In Your Mind"
Columbia*	KC-34112	"The Troublemaker"
Columbia	KC-34695	"To Lefty from Willie"
Columbia	JC-35305	"Stardust"

* Records now available through record companies and record distributors; those without an asterisk can only be found in rare instances.

Columbia	JC-35642	"Willie and Family Live"
Columbia	KC-236064	"Willie Nelson and Leon Russell—One for the Road"
Columbia	JC-36188	"Willie Nelson Sings Kristoferson"
Columbia	JC-36189	"Willie Nelson—Pretty Papers"
Plantation*	PLP-24	"Willie Nelson and His Friends"
RCA*	APLI-1487	"Willie Nelson Live" (Reissue of most of "Country Music Concert" RCA-LSP 3659)
RCA*	APLI-2210	"Willie/Before His Time"

Willie also appears as a featured artist on the following albums:

Atlantic	SD-7310	"Tracy Nelson" (Willie & Tracy sing "After The Fire Is Gone")
Epic*	PE-33851	"Swans Against the Sun" (Michael Murphey)
RCA	VPS-6037	"This Is the Nashville Sound"
RCA	VPS-6048	"Best of a Great Year, Vol. I"
RCA-Camden	ADL2-0782	"50 Years of Country Music"
RCA*	APL1-0539	"This Time" (Waylon Jennings)
Starday	STR-430	"Country Hall Of Fame"
Sunset	SNS-5283	"Country Get-Together"
Sunset	SNS-5290	"More Country Gold"
United Artists	UA-LA413-E	"Very Best of Country Gold, Vol. II"
RCA	CPL3-0697	"Great Country Hits of the Year"
RCA	LSP-4793	"Wishing You a Merry Christmas"
RCA*	APLI-1520	"Mackintosh and T.J."
Diplomat	DS2408	"Great Stars of Country & Western, Vol. II"

45 RPM records which are currently available include:

RCA Victor	447-0891	"The Party's Over"/"Bring Me Sunshine"
RCA Victor	447-0945	"Good Hearted Woman"/"Sweet Dream Woman" (Waylon Jennings)
RCA Victor	PB-10429	"Fire and Rain"/"I'm a Memory"
RCA Victor	PB-10461	"Pretty Papers"/"What a Merry Christmas This Could Be"
Atlantic	ATC-13178	"Shotgun Willie"/"I Still Can't Believe You're Gone"
Atlantic	ATC 13179	"After the Fire is Gone"/"Bloody Mary Morning"
Atlantic	ATC 3228	"Pick Up the Tempo"/"Sister's Coming Home"
Columbia	COL 3-10176	"Blue Eyes Crying in the Rain"/"Bandera"
Columbia	COL 3-10275	"Remember Me"/"Time of the Preacher"
United Artists	UA-XW771-Y	"The Last Letter"/"There Goes a Man"
RCA Victor	PB-10591	"I Gotta Get Drunk"/"Summer of Roses"
Columbia	3-10327	"I'd Have to Be Crazy"/"Amazing Grace"
Columbia	3-10383	"If You've Got the Money, I've Got the Time"/"The Sound in Your Mind"

* Records now available through record companies and record distributors; those without an asterisk can only be found in rare instances.